Seeing into the Golden Eyes of Buddha

◆

Herman Wong

PublishAmerica
Baltimore

Hardcover 978-1-4512-9676-1
Softcover 978-1-4512-9677-8
PUBLISHED BY PUBLISHAMERICA, LLLP
www.publishamerica.com
Baltimore

Printed in the United States of America

Image and the Oracle (Moving Line Interpretation)

The Image

This is the Image of T'ai - Peace

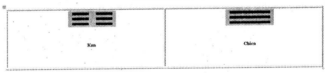

Kun

Chien

The Significance of the Image

Chien, who moves upwards, is below Kun, who moves downwards, is above. Hence this is a perfectly harmonious state when both Yang and Yin merge together in harmony. This signifies that heaven has descended on the earth, and their power has united in deep harmony. Peace and prosperity reigns in all the nook and corners of the earth.

The Judgment

The Heaven descends
The Earth ascends
Heaven and Earth marry
Within each mass
Peace and prosperity for all.

Table of Contents

Blessings,

Herman Wong.

Preface

This book is about awakening the soul and finding eternal peace within your heart. If you wish to know or learn how to awaken your kind, compassionate soul, this book may serve as a guide to what you seek.

For centuries, people have been searching for and seeking help, hoping to release the suppressions and emotions within and, at the same time, wondering how they can find release from their pains and sorrows in the world within and without.

Perhaps, I begin with these prophetic words:

Life, events and circumstances are unpredictable and unpreventable.

Life is dynamic: joy, happiness, or sadness and misfortune can be perceived everywhere.

They are only brought to an end when life has ended.

Pains and sorrows will also come to a close.

Being kind and compassionate to others is the only way.

Pray for forgiveness for our faults towards others.

Wish well in Buddha's heart.

Align your desire, intentions and actions with the Universal Source.

Gaining life improvement and consciously unite with the Source, becoming one.

We breathe in and exhale and relinquish the past moment, as it is impermanent in its spiritual significance. Thus, we observe consciously the endless instant and accommodate the person we are becoming and accept this entire process. We are mindful of the timeless present and become intimately conscious of the resonating facility of life.

When we close ourselves to others, then we are no longer open in our hearts to welcome others to love and help each other. That is, we are holding back in ourselves and that we are withdrawing can be seen and felt through the expressions on our faces. These unkind emotions can be eliminated through practice, kindness and compassion, through meditation and mind-training to shut off unwanted desires that are hidden within and release them to the consciousness in the here and now so that we live life with integrity and compassion.

Through the practice of meditation, focused on kindness and compassion, we can train our minds to quiet our consciousness by thinking and focusing on giving love to each other and being there for others, without thinking of ourselves first: in this way, we will avoid destructive thinking. It is through meditation that we become detached from everything and let confusion and troubles go, aiming at refreshment. This allows you to open the channel of your inner consciousness to align with the physical self. Meditation withdraws you temporarily from the physical world and allows you to connect and align with the spiritual realm.

Through conscious connection with the Universal Source, we understand that separation from each other is not real. Since the beginning of creation, we misunderstood the truth in our thoughts and feel a sense of separation from the Source and others. In fact, we are always consciously connected with one another through the power of collective consciousness: hence, our minds are connected; therefore, we can feel others' pains and sorrows. We could widen our compassion to let ourselves feel what it is like to be in their shoes. Although we cannot tell what others should do, by focusing and offering our thoughts positively for long enough, we can influence the thoughts of others so that they think positively, reducing negative emotions in their minds. That is the influence you can offer others.

Before we can offer help to heal others' wounds, we must heal our own hearts within. To heal our inner wound, we must repeatedly forgive ourselves and give ourselves unlimited love and kindness so that, in turn, we can send unconditional love to others. If we can heal our own wounds and try to understand our own pains and sorrows, then we will able to see others' pains through the filter of others and be more than willing to offer help. True kindheartedness does not judge or discriminate about who we should help, but treats and respects everyone equally with love and care.

Throughout our daily practice of kindness and compassion, we can help to relieve stress and bring practical help to our daily living. We can bring experience to our path and use it as an awakening tool for our aptitudes, our love, our kindness and our ability to start afresh, and then as we continue to make changes as we transform.

In one winter month of 2005, I shut off everything and focused on practicing meditation to connect to the inner consciousness and train the mind to compassion and kindness. The purpose of this meditation was to be awakened to the frustration and difficulties of my daily life activities. During meditation, I perceived solutions that I could apply in all circumstances and situations, especially those in which I usually prefer to use blame or ignorance. That is, I perceive it as a chance, and open my mind to make transformations and learn to crave positive emotional thoughts that I find from within.

Even though, in the beginning, I did not know how meditation could transform my life, gradually I saw and realized that my whole attitude has changed regarding my path and life purpose on Earth. I could relate to it, after months practicing compassion and kindness, as a result of being on the path of unconditional compassionate living. This could be reflected on after I had gone through difficult times of darkness in the past. I benefited from it, as it opened and relaxed me. I began to understand life is dynamic and continued to love myself, and remembered that I am so important in the Divine consciousness. The benefit is a continuum, designed to extend the kindness and benevolence to others.

Chapter One
Awakening compassion

If we understand how the Universe works, then we realize we have received everything we need. There is no need to fearing a lack. All we need to do is feel good and believe that all things are possible and available in the creative consciousness. That idea prevents us from constantly thinking of scarcity and clinging to our jealousy of others' wealth. It is like a dark cloud that temporarily blocks the sun and all we see is darkness. But, in fact, we did not see the whole picture of warmth and comfort that is right here in the now. This is who we really are. We cannot see clearly when we are one blink of an eye away from being fully conscious or awake.

Looking at ourselves through a transition glass is very different from following our usual habits. From this perspective, you do not need to change: you can do and feel whatever you like, and perhaps you are still a good candidate for enlightenment. You understand the life cycle of rebirth and human desire, and suffering is transcended. You can feel the world is full of suffering and that feeling is within you. There is also richness in small things that we like or dislike and so we do not desire them. The things that we love are clearly about ourselves, from within us so that we feel some sense of inspiration or satisfaction: that is our wealth. We are proud of recognizing who-we-really-are: a spiritual being that allows us manifest many positive things to ourselves and to benefit others.

To attain spiritual awakening you can stay where you are and make transformations to get where you want to be. You will feel the difference after you practice calmness and meditation within. If you are an angry person, you may need to use all your anger in your life as a means to awaken your compassion. Through meditation, you will learn how to accept yourself, and how to relate directly to pain and suffering, how accept painful experiences as a part of your life and stop running away from that.

When we talk about compassion, this immediately connects our minds to love and caring; it naturally brings up the point that we should cooperate with others and care for others. The reason we are not there for others is because we do not feel love for ourselves and remember ourselves. Therefore, we run away from helping others and escape as far away as we can to avoid being asked for help.

Because we escape, we miss emerging at the right place at the right time. We keep missing something better happening at that moment. Yet, if we can catch the right moment, we realize that it is unique and completely new and only happens once and is never repeated. One can appreciate and celebrate every moment and that moment is the most sacred. That moment is most enormous and whole, and there is nothing extra.

When we sit down quietly and contemplate the pain that we have within and we have the boldness to face it all, then we eliminate fear, build courage and have confidence like a warrior:

we are willing to feel the pain of others and ultimately offer genuine help to them. Because we are brave and bold enough to face pain, then we realize that our pains are similar to theirs.

Through practice, meditation awakens the power within us, and our trust that the knowledge, wisdom and benevolence we need are already inside us. The Inner Child/Soul helps us to understand our weaknesses and strengths, our truthfulness, tolerance, integrity and enthusiasm, our anger, frustration, aggression, hatred, lack of awareness, love and wisdom.

The reason that we do not love each other, the reason that we hate and bring harm to others and do not care about other people's lives, that the planet is warming and animals are not doing well is because we lack care and only want to satisfy individual needs and interests. The causes are a lack of trust and love, a failure to remember ourselves and that there is no tranquility felt within. Therefore, to practice meditation helps us to attain inner calmness and that is the key that helps us to understand and know ourselves and continue to live life fearlessly, healthily and peacefully.

Now, find a quiet place to sit down begin your meditation session. You must sit straight with your legs crossed and at this stage keep your eyes open. Put your hands on your thighs. Then, you must be aware of your breathing, as the breath goes in and out. You can take a long deep breath: inhale and exhale. Next, you must completely relax your whole body. You simply guide yourself to be in the present, be aware of your breath, and be aware of your surroundings, the noise and almost everything around you. You do not need to reject what is coming to you, but be present at the moment while you sit still and are aware of the breath going out.

You realize different thoughts are still running through your mind: some are unexpected and ones that occurred in the past continue to surface. Your mind still wanders off to many things whether you want it to or not. You still think positive or negative emotional thoughts. It gives them a chance to parade out in front of you at this quiet moment. Whether your thoughts are recalled/retrieved from memories or are worries about your life, whether you think how well you are doing, or your thoughts are of your spiritual life, or pleasing thoughts such as your accomplishments and achievements, or many other thoughts that will come to you expected or unexpected, you must not judge what comes to you: let it pass through and do that quietly, smoothly and with calmness.

You continue to breathe in and out, you fill the room with your breathing and let your breath enter into the empty space. You remain aware of what your surroundings are, within and without you. Then, you realize all of sudden that you entered into the gap of a sacred place that is so profound and peaceful, waiting for you to embrace it. You thought you entered into the gap of conscious connection with the Source. But, this has not yet happened as your mind still wanders off and you are thinking again! This time you are annoyed with your thoughts and give yourself a hard time. You must be patient and gentle with yourself. You need to focus on an opportunity to develop kindness and compassion for yourself. You tell yourself everything is fine. You simply let the unwanted desire go and it will fade away when you pay no attention to what is bothering you at the moment during meditation. You can see it that is reflected in your true self and you accept it, ready to make the changes in your real life.

Although what you perceive in your mind's eye during meditation is painful, it starts to heal when you stop hiding your real self. It is healing to know that all these years you are not genuinely yourself; you are living in a delusion with the illusion of fear in the way you closed and shut off yourself, judged others and did things that are considered to be unacceptable by others and yourself. You also find out the other side of you is kind and caring and compassionate. You are now thinking more positively and are ready to make the change you need in the real world. You begin awakening a transformation to become a different person filled with compassion with kindness to others, but you must start with yourself.

When you return to the real world, you continue training your mind through meditation. You can accept and make friends with what is considered as bad in yourself and by others. By the same token, you are learning to treasure what is generally considered to be good. If you are to live in this way, something in you that has been buried for a long time begins to mature. You have just awakened your spiritual heart. It is something that has always been there, but you just did not realize its existence.

It is as if you bought a new home and, although you do not know it, right under the ground where you lived was a hidden treasure. That treasure is you awakening your own Inner Soul. Your confusion about who-you-really-are comes from not knowing that the treasure is right there, but you were always looking for it somewhere else. One night you wake up and realize all you have been seeking for—joy and happiness—were in a different place. You should know better: the pot of gold is right there and patiently waiting for you all along with no complaint.

When you awaken, you hold different attitudes towards unwanted things: if it is painful you are more than willing to endure it, but also let it open your heart and soften you. You learn to accept and embrace it.

However, if an experience is pleasant you want to maintain and hold it for a very long time. You should allow this delightful experience to be shared with other people and wish them to have the same moment you are experiencing. Share the wealth with others, and be generous with your joy and happiness. Detach from what you want and offer help to the most needy, share your insights and knowledge. Do not let fear overwhelm you so you believe in scarcity and become attached to things, but share them.

Whether you seek a release from your pains or gain pleasure through mind-training, come to let your experiences be as they are without trying to change or push them away. Both pain and pleasure are an unavoidable part of our lives and are the key element to awaken our Inner Being or spiritual heart.

It is said that in order to thrive in your endeavor, you must help others gain success before you can gain victory yourself. This eliminates the ego-concept: "Me first and be careless of others". That kind of attitude is the main cause of all failure and pain.

The idea is to eliminate gaining victory as the most important thing in your mind. Your concerns and interest guides your heart: only care for yourselves and ignore others. Hence, nothing can get through to change how you think of others. In the short run, maybe you cannot see any immediate difference, but, in a long term, you become self-interested and egoistic, and totally ignore the welfare of other people, and continue to grab all you can to yourself. When people ask for your help you say to them, "If I help you, what do I benefit from it?" You become a very greedy, jealous and supremely egotistical person. Unknowingly, you turn to your own comfort in selfishness with a wounded heart in a smaller world. Your love and caring characteristics totally vanish into the thin air. Think about it: do you really gain anything?

On the other hand, when you think about helping others to

succeed, you are connected to your Inner Soul. Something opens your heart to touch the life of others. This something is what you have all the time, but now you activate it again. Because you have never felt that before, you are afraid and want it to stop and never feel it again. The contact was so soft. But, as you still try to deactivate it, instead you make it more active. Then, you decide to let it alone.

In the physical world, we all want to win and gain victory and sweep defeat under the rug. That is how we end up by imprisoning ourselves with the confusion of not knowing that we have limitless wealth, and the confusion becomes deeper each time we win and get more excited and become more ambitious. You think that you are invincible, you are undefeated: that's victory.

The truth is, we cannot win all the time and there is no permanent winner. Believing that you can have victory all the time is an illusion: a new-comer arises all the time. Winning and losing just comes and goes. But, if you let things go, you actually let fresh air replace the old, you allow your Inner Source to guide you where it needs to be.

If you think you can win all the time, God will defeat you so that you have tasted what losing means. You then will open your heart to accept defeat is a natural process and always be aware that, at the end, nobody wins it all.

You always feel unintelligent, you are too fat and not smart enough. You have this inner-dialogue with yourself, "Nobody loves me, I am always a loner". That all comes under the label of "loser", the defeat of ego. You do not always want to be the real "you". You cannot accept that God has created you and cannot change. However, we can never connect with our inner-wealth if we always want to be someone else and look different.

On the other hand, when you let go of winning and give it to others instead of keeping it to yourself, there is a sense of sharing the joyful aspect of your life. You lose something, but gain something more important you do, such as the way you look at the mirror. You have released the weight on your shoulders. You feel alive, happier, as if you were falling in love. When the seasons change, you begin to notice the snow falling for the very first time and you enjoy it. With anything that you want, you begin to develop the attitude of sharing wealth with others and that eliminates the scarcity and fearful feeling around you.

When we work without fear, we can relate with joy and happiness and see how those things can transform us fully and completely. When we work well within normal life, we will be transformed on the path of awakening.

Chapter Two
Awakened Heart

The practice of meditation helps us to develop and trust our awakened heart, the heart of Bodhictitta. If we could realize the richness in our heart, then our consciousness of heavy burdens would be banished and our sense of curiosity would rise.

The heart of Bodhictitta contains three qualities: compassion, openness, and clarity. They blend to become one quality, called Bodhictitta.

Bodhictitta is our spiritual heart: you could not actually see or touch it. It is a symbolic heart that is hidden within us. You look within and all you find is the awakened heart that guides your daily living.

What is Bodhictitta? You may need to seek out your own way to find out its meaning in your own lives. Bodhictitta is capable of softening a person's heart and fearful mind and changing them into joyful aspects of one's being. That is, we can continue to let circumstances harden and upset us so that we become more resentful, or we can allow them soften us, making us become more open and less scared. We always have a choice regarding what to do.

Bodhichitta is an associate, together with compassion, that allows us to share our pain with others. Without realizing it, we continually block ourselves from this pain within because it scares us. We build up walls and protective shields for the reason that we fear getting hurt. These walls we setup are covered by negative emotions such as anger, hatred, jealousy, envy, fear, worry, doubt, indecision, arrogance, and pride. But, our innate ability to love and to care about things, allows us to break the barriers of these walls. It opens the barriers that we created when we were afraid. Through the practice of meditation and mind-training, we learn to discover this gap. We then enter into this opening to grab that vulnerable moment which is love, compassion, thankfulness, loneliness, and lack— to awaken Bodhichitta.

Now, consider that this life is dream, so death is also dream. In other words, all situations are a passing memory.

For example, you went for a walk this morning, but now it is a passing event only in your memory. Indeed, every situation and circumstance is a passing memory. In our lives we have experienced many recurring events—we have eaten many meals, spent many hours with friends and family, spent many hours driving to work and back home: these things have been repeated and recurred many times. All these events bring up some good and bad memories. Once it was real and now it transformed into a past memory.

It is as if I wonder: do I write this book or do I dream and write at the same time? Dreams are just as true as we believe waking reality to be. So, you could begin to contemplate the fact that perhaps things are not as real or reliable as they seem.

Sometimes you just have this experience automatically or it

happens to you in your dream. It happens when you are lost in the desert by yourself: a mirage occurs that confuses you. You are not sure whether what is present in front of you is real or an illusion. You thought you saw a stream of water, but in fact it is not real. It is all imagination in your dream. Dreams can make our world feel so much bigger, since in a dreaming experience our world is limitless and has no ending. Dreams can last forever until you awake to reality in real time. Just like Buddha, we like to find out the basic truth about our life. But are we capable of exposing what's going on? The Buddha's answer is, "yes, we can." But, we need to find this out through meditation, due to our confusion, because we do not understand how our mind works. Through meditation we can stabilize and strengthen our mind. We are able to observe what is happening in our mind, giving us a chance to see a clear picture of truthfulness constantly. During meditation, we can relax and see a bigger prospective rather than thinking of limitations.

A long-term meditation can make our mind more stable and more strengthened. Meditation is open to everyone and anyone can do. It does not involve a particular spiritual tradition. It helps you undo your confusion and learn to become a responsible person and use your mind wisely: it does not matter what beliefs you hold.

Meditation helps us create a peaceful state and lets our mind be as it is to begin with. This does not mean that we ignore things. It means that we keep our mind in the same place without wondering around and constantly changing. Meditation gives you the effect of calm and enduring peace.

It is true that our mind is not always calm and enduringly peaceful. We see pain and problems in our mind. It is no big deal. We could all just cheer up by regarding that all is happening as a dream. Believe whatever happens as if it were in our dreams, becoming and passing into memory.

Have you ever tried to catch the beginning, middle and end of every thought? You obviously find it does seem to have beginning, middle and end. Those parts certainly are there. Perhaps you are talking to yourself: you are creating your own uniqueness, your own planet, your own sense of problems, your own sense of contentment and your own sense of recurrent thought. But, thoughts are still there, always shifting. Every situation, word, thought and even emotion can easily become a passing memory. It is like when water turns into an ice cube: you can never catch that precise moment. You know it was water, because you could drink it, but you cannot see exactly when one thing changes into other. Everything happens like that: we cannot catch the right moment unless the thing turns into stillness, then we might have a chance to witness that precise moment. However, once that moment has passed, we can never get it back. It becomes a past memory.

Have you ever gotten a feeling which was so outrageous and hurtful, and then all of sudden you just drop it? You just let it go as if it has nothing happened. You feel very calm and peaceful within. Then, you wonder why you made such a big deal out of nothing. Similarly, it is as if one day you woke and decided to buy a thirteen-inch notebook from Dell. You were so excited about buying it and looked at their website and the notebook. You looked at the configuration of the notebook and loved it. You wanted the notebook badly. Then, a few hours later, you do not know what went wrong, but the feeling's gone and you can't get it back. We all know the feeling of how we take things seriously and then realize that we are making a lot out of nothing, especially when at the end we decided not go ahead.

Often we find ourselves so tense, uptight and upset about

small things. This kind of feeling is quite normal, but you must not let it last for the whole day, and remember to cheer up. You must not let this kind of negative feeling hurt yourself for nothing. If you continue doing it, you are working against yourself. Remember, when you find yourself upset and tense, do not forget to cheer up. It will bring calmness and kindness to you and you will feel that you are the candidate of Bodhichitta—the compassionate and open and lovely heart of Bodhichitta.

Kindness and calmness in our practice and in our daily meditation help us to awaken and reconnect with Bodhichitta. It is in order to remember something. It is as though we lost something, then we found it again. It helps to remind us that kindness, compassion and openness is what we really are. To practice Bodhichitta is to be reconnected to our original quality of cheerful consciousness and feel the inner joy and apply it to our daily practice of living.

To practice meditation is the best way to bring the effect you always want and encourage you to be gentle and kind to yourself and always remember to love yourself for who you really are. Meditation will soften everything from within to be gentle and kind. Then, when you let the whole thing become soft, you exhale out and the breathing dissolves out into the air with softness. You are simply relaxing externally with your breath. Practice inhaling and exhaling: exercise helps you to relax your whole body and have completely forgotten the stress of the moment. It brings back the calmness and tranquility that you had a moment ago and reconnects you with Bodhichitta to cheer you up in your practice and your life.

Do not worry about achieving anything in your mind, but label it as positive or negative thinking and apply it later. If there is anything you do not want, just let it go and release it into the thin air. Do not be too concerned about it. The negative feelings will dissolve and vanish into space. They won't hurt you unless you allow yourself and desire to contemplate about them. It all will pass and transform into past memory. When you finish that session of meditation, you will feel fresh with positive emotional thoughts in the mind and obviously you would like to utilize what you observe within and apply it in your real time so that you will benefit from it.

Thoughts come and go: you do not need to hold onto any thought at all. You simply have to let go when the thought has left you. You have to just let it be and let the thoughts go and they will come up again and you will see them for what they are. It is not that serious that you lost that thought. You can take it easy, cheer up and let it be. Thought is like a dream, it will pass you and you simply free it and move on to your next thought and some other thoughts that come to you. You will always receive inspiration from your thoughts and you will never lose thoughts. Thought has no end and no beginning. Thoughts are like your dreams. You miss that moment and can never catch it again. Do not regret it, but continue to feel good and that it's no big deal. It is only a thought and will come back to you some time. Get a better thought to fill the gap if you think it will make you feel better, or forget about it.

The most important thing is to be connected with your Bodhichitta heart within and be open, receptive and give the highest quality of your mind so that there is no need to shut off your vulnerable thoughts and believe they will fade away by themselves. Then, you let that go and you do not need to think it again.

During meditation, you must relax: there's no way anything bad will happen. Wherever you find yourself, just relax. Relax your whole body, every organ, every cell, every blood vessel and most importantly your mind. The form and structure are already there and you simply move within that good feeling and gentleness. That's how you awaken and connect your heart.

Chapter Three
Who am I?

Before I graduated and obtained my degree in metaphysics, I was asked to present a class for two and a half hours on a topic I freely selected, and I had to present in a way applicable to the class. At the end of my presentation, people who listened to what I was saying agreed with it in some way if they adopted my ideas.

Who are you? I am a spiritual being that comes from the Universal Source, the Mind of God. The Source is my maker. The living spirit dwells within me to guide my journey on Earth. The physical body is only temporary, but the spirit is real, dynamic and infinite. The physical body is a refuge or a temple for my soul. This allows the spirit within to accompany me while I learn lessons, have experiences and fulfill my spiritual journey on Earth right to the end.

The spirit knows everything I need to accomplish my goals and achieve my desires while I undertake my journey on Earth. Hence, everything is sustained and can be obtained through the power of inner-most thought. Through the power of planting my thought seeds inside and having optimistic emotions and creative visualization in my mind's eye, the subconscious mind later on transcends these visualized pictures into the Universe and will meet with other conscious thoughts: when energy becomes mature and returns to the physical world, the subliminal mind translates that powerful energy into language the conscious mind can understand. Consequently, the mind automatically transforms such powerful dynamic energy into coherent physical actions through you and opens the inner doorway of your desires into the life of blessedness in the outer world as the resolution to the desires you want to achieve and bring to physical reality someday.

Who is this "I"? Where did it come from? What is your social identity? Who is this me? Why is it the concern for the "I" so important? This I-concept is made up of thoughts in the mind to make you feel you are so important, so distinguished, so superior to others. In fact, this idea of who you are is created by the ego's attitudes and concepts. It is recorded in memory and can be retrieved in the subconscious mind.

When you have the ego around you, the kind heart cannot connect with you. You are temporarily disconnected from reality in the dream world of self-seeking. You are shielded and hosted by the ego and move further away from real reality. You are distant from comfort and security and continue to create a new pattern you think is right for you. You do not make things more solid, rather you build on a shaky ground with no foundations. You enter the dimension of the unknown and do not know what the future holds for you. You do not live in the now, but live in a world of illusion which you thought could get something that the ego promises to get you some day.

This is not what you really want in your heart or how you usually go about things, it is just that you had not noticed the difference between reality and illusion as the ego causes you to be unaware of things that can happen. You are an emotional being who can be easily influenced and affected by the environment and feel insecure or restless. Only by connecting the heart within can you have calmness and tranquility so that you can stand on the ground and feel safe and secure again. Joy and happiness come from that. Joy arises deep from within: the joy of the Infinite Being.

Examine the nature of unconsciousness, of who we are. Simply examine the nature of who has the insight—contemplation. The "I' possesses this insight, but has frozen in time and space and needs to be awakened. Who is doing all the thinking? Thoughts come from the Universal Source, then are translated by the subconscious, converted into the language the conscious mind can understand—it is always direct and produced by the physical mind converting it into the real world. Therefore, everything is shifting all the time, we think we can repair and fix problems. If we can catch the dilemma, then we can fix it or whoever comes up with a solid conclusion. Just let it go, cheer up and being kind and gentle to yourself and do not take it seriously. You can make your own decisions or you can let your awakened heart within decide for you. You are always given choices and will never be left alone without being allowed to decide. You make your own decision and no one can decide for you. If you can't make a steadfast decision, you simply let go and everything will fall into place: lighten up, observe and stay consciousness and positive and believe everything will transform into the desire you always want. You must stay in consciousness, and connect in the now, then everything is available to you. You are shown how to liberate yourself from craving in the mind, enter into enlightened states of consciousness and sustain them in your daily living.

Now, who am I? I am not my five physical senses, which are smell, touch, sight, hearing and feel. I am not the blood vessels, cells, body, heart, organs, and even my own thoughts. I am actually a spiritual being dwelling in a physical body to assist you (the self) walking on a spiritual journey on Earth. I am just who I am and nothing else. The awareness is that I am a spirit. It is when the mind emerges that the self disappears. When the self emerges, then the mind is silent. Thoughts arise from the spiritual heart. When the mind appears, thoughts are not filtered and contain selfish thoughts concerning only the "I" which do not care for others. Thoughts are inspired by the Universal Source so that you can attain peace within.

In the physical world, do you introduce yourself as who you are? For instance: I am a doctor, I am a student, I am the President of the United States of America, or I am whatever you are in your current situation. I also have a distinguished character, attitude, personality, something you like or dislike. I like the color blue, I like to eat Japanese food, I like to write and give speeches. It is important for you to know that the "I am" attributes will follow you anywhere, wherever you go for the rest of your life.

In order to understand who you really are in the real world, we also need to study the true nature reflected in your world or secret world. Your secret world contains your thoughts, beliefs, emotions, and opinions and can be expressed by the things you do, your movements, your decisions, and even particular clothing you like to wear and the surroundings where you live. It is all about you and no one else. Your personality is also reflected in how you decorate your home, the color of the walls in your home, your pictures and collections. What those items represent during the time of your collection is that they make you happy, joyful or bring sad memories. The kinds of clothes you like to wear are expensive or simply comfortable. The kinds of friends you have are supportive or distant, and what are the kinds of book you like to read? These show the way that others see who you are in the material world. Your net worth is also considered and counted as a part of your attributes so that you can be trusted as you are introduced to others and relate to the world that is around you.

Your body is the temple for your soul, within which your spirit dwells; it is a tool where your soul guides your journey, and it walks on the spiritual path on Earth with you until the end. So you are more than just the physical body, but have a soul dwelling within that recognizes you as a spiritual being. You only use your body once, but your soul probably evolved from many lives before it entered to your body. Therefore, you must look after your body and treat it very well. In fact, it is only the human body, mind and spirit that reveals the unknowable, unique being in a tangible form.

Now, it goes back to life is but a dream. In a dream, you exist in a certain world. Your identity in a dream may not reflect your character or personality in your waking world. On your dream stage, you have friends, as well as enemies. Some of these may be a reflection of people you know in the waking hours; others may be the combination of characters that you know or meet on a daily basis and, of course, yourself. Nonetheless, all these characters are all in one—you. That means that in a dream you are made into many personalities and characters, but they are only images and reflect one personality—it is all about you. In a dream state, you can act and express yourself freely, carrying out the freedom of pure creative consciousness in your own true nature. You reveal the true nature of you, the hidden secret of your world can also be disclosed in your dream.

Finally, when you are conscious of who you are, you are also more conscious and aware of how you are thinking, speaking and acting. You will give thought in whatever you do to ensure you cannot hurt anybody. Self-knowledge gives you objective insight to purify your thoughts, words, actions, and every attribute that is related to you, all at the same time. You will love yourself as you begin to understand yourself and know yourself as a unique person: there is only one you and never compare yourself to anyone, because your uniqueness is different from others. You live once, but your soul will last forever. You respect, accept, love and are compassionate to yourself and others. You will live a joyful and tranquil life on Earth.

Chapter Four
Suffering

Sarnath: "Look deeply into the nature of suffering to see the causes of suffering and the way out."

The Buddha Siddhartha recognized at a very young age that suffering exists and tried to find out why it exists. We are also aware of suffering and learning to reduce the globe's suffering as much as possible. Suffering is always there, around us, in our surroundings, within and without us and the only thing we can do is to discover a way to transform it into peace and tranquility.

God created the planet Earth and two humans Adam and Eve, and animals and plants and everything in it in six consecutive days. He instructed the two humans that "the tree of the knowledge of good and evil you shall not eat, for in the day that you eat of it you shall surely die" Genesis 2:17.

However, Adam and Eve disobeyed the order from the creator. God kept his word: from then on all humans suffered and died and no one is above life. God was upset, but he loves us and yet his command must be carried out; therefore, we suffer from sickness and death. Our original fault has a consequence, and the price must be paid for our rebellion against God. If our ancestors had not made that serious blunder, then we would not value the love of God and realize it is so precious and great and He loves us all.

Life is suffering: that is true. There are reasons for suffering and there is an end to suffering. What causes suffering is either known or unknown to us. Perhaps before we entered into this birth, we signed an accord with the creator that we agreed voluntary to experience what suffering is like. So, immediately you entered here you began to experience different kinds of suffering: whether it is pleasant or unpleasant you must endure and keep it going until the end. Although suffering is real, we still can find a path to ease our pains and suffering so that our lives are easier and we feel less pain while we continue our journey and lessons on Earth.

Life begins with birth, then we grow old and death is the ultimate destination. Rebirth is an option, if we choose to return. Because life contains suffering, there must be something that causes our suffering. It could be illness, disease, struggles or pain. These could be the reasons that we see deeply into the nature of suffering in life and, when the end comes, we return to dust.

Suffering is not pessimistic, but rather a practical path in our approach to life. For example, if you fell from a horse and injured your spinal cord, then you suffered tremendous pain in your back. You temporarily feel enormous pain as a result of falling from a horse. It is an accident which is not predicable and preventable. You cannot blame anyone, but accept it as an incident. It is a practical, problem-solving approach life. Suffering is part of the healing process in life. There's always a way to reduce your suffering from financial situations to poor health and most painful experience ever.

The best way to approach suffering is face the dilemma, to see the cause of suffering and seek the way out. But, most of us are afraid to face the stress and would rather not see it or do not accept the pain is real. However, the sooner you accept and acknowledge the pain and suffering, the sooner you treat it with joy and happiness. That way—by understanding it—we can discover its cause and bring an end to it. If you have confidence, you know your body is suffering, but the soul (self) has not suffered. You have fed your body with consistent stress and become disconnected from the self, but when you let go and detach your body and emotions from painful memories in the past, then you will know what it's like to be totally liberated from suffering.

On the other hand, suffering may not even be in your body, but due to clinging on to past memories of being damaged by someone: you cling on to aggressive behavior or bad habits, you cling on to your financial lost or setback, you cling on to a past relationship that does not exist anymore and many other reasons that may cause you pain and suffering and snatch away the joy and happiness you deserve. However, when you free yourself from clinging onto something, it will lead to the total benefit of permanent joy and happiness.

So, you discontinue hugging suffering. You eliminate the physical pain that causes you mental pain. When you become attached to the illness and worry that aging and death may occur, this will cause more mental stresses. You see, if you do not stop the suffering and get it under control, then you become the sufferer and trap yourself. When you realize your true identity and the capacity of who-you-really-are, then you are not afraid of being sick, aging, and death. You know death is an illusion and your soul will never expire. That automatically eliminates your illusion of the fear of life and death. It gives you the degree of peace that you feel within.

When discussing suffering, is it correct to say that less privileged people suffer more than the privileged class in society? Suffering does not just befall less privileged people, but privileged people too. They too will suffer painful experiences, setbacks and disappointments, illness and death. Perhaps the noises of suffering from the under privileged class are louder than from the privileged class. The privileged people can easily take care of everything, yet, at the end, no one is above suffering or death. The slogan says, "Long live the King, but the King is dead."

Although suffering is unavoidable, we can practice compassion and kindness, giving to the needy and offering professional services to others, chanting God's names and mantra and practicing meditation of mindfulness, emptiness, openness, and selfishness to attain calmness and peace within. We can learn to maintain our awareness that each thing we do in our daily life may somehow help us to reduce our pain and sorrows and to release the size of the ego in order achieve greater realization.

The basic principle of suffering is that all is suffering, but, to reduce suffering, one must eliminate attachment and selfish desire. When one reaches the undesired state of Nirvana, it brings an end to suffering; that is an individual is desireless and consciousness comes to an end. To attain Nirvana, one must overcome hatred, envy, greed and ignorance. One must accept imperfection. One must eliminate or abandon a bad character and replace it with one of good quality and endorse good deed. One must live a reasonable quality of life and avoid bad actions towards others or causing harm to others. One must eliminate hateful intentions, dishonesty, stealing, and killing. One must be vigilant in the use of thought and words in speech. Ultimately, an individual must seek their own goals and use their efforts to reduce suffering and find a way out.

Chapter Five
Living in the world of illusion

We know of the information that we have about the external world by means of our five senses: what our eyes see, our ears hear, our nose smells, our tongue tastes and our hands feel. We depended on those five senses since birth: the way we are is limited by what is presented by these senses. Everything we see, touch, smell, hear and taste in the external world is only an electrical signal in our brain. For instance, we see an eagle in the external world. In reality this world is not in the external world but is an electrical signal in our brain. So, if the sight nerve traveling to the brain is disconnected we do not see the bird again. Simply, it is an electrical signal translated by the brain.

The external world is an illusion. Its existence is just the image translated in our brain; when the electrical nerve signal is disconnected we cannot see it and the external world disappears from us. Our world is like a hologram: very vivid and very solid, but this is only when we receive the signal in our brain telling us that we see the material world. It would be ridiculous to say it is not real or it was not there. Everything we hear is an echo back

HERMAN WONG

from the emptiness, the sound is real, but it is the echo of emptiness. The sound you hear is the electrical signal you receive from the brain converted into a sound wave so you can hear.

Similarly anything you label as good or bad, happy and sad, all thoughts can vanish into emptiness and leave no trace, so you retrieve or now you see an eagle flying into deep sky. For example, you watch movie in a room but in fact the room is in your brain; however, when the nerve's electrical signal tells you about the room you are watching movie in, the brain is blocked so you cannot see the room. Therefore, all you see is a vivid illusion: it looks real but is there and then, all of a sudden, it is not there. When the electrical signal in the brain is reconnected again, the room's image emerges again.

To further explain this illusion, it usually seems to appear in young children's minds. In their world, they like to imagine things which are not so solid. But, they see them as real, they act as though holding an object in their hands and they can play by themselves through imagining things. They have a lot of fun and they seem to live in a different dimension, out of touch. It is so innocent, profound and perfect. Then, all of sudden, they just drop it and imagination ceases. It is not solid at all, but vivid imagination in the mind's experience in the external world through the power of thought.

It is like the way you experience, view and attain the encouragement of meditation through relaxation, so that the whole atmosphere of your experience just starts to come to you. However, how things are cannot be taught—no one can give you that experience. You simply must experience and practice to achieve it yourself. It is as though you want to attain enlightenment, you must seek to discover it yourself. For instance, you are in a boat, but you need a push to cross the river to the other side. Without that force you will never really get to the seashore. Enlightenment is the end of suffering. You need to be in the present and find yourself. Your mind must still be in order to attain this goal, then, through meditation, you can gain awareness of your own being and abide in that internal state of feeling of recognition that is enlightenment.

Remember all things are an illusion in the external world: try to encourage yourself not to feel so strongly about good or bad feelings in the mind and do not walk on their battle-field. In fact, parts of ourselves are good and evil and parts of ourselves are joyful and happy.

The reality is that, for millions of years, good and evil have been at war with each other. This war will never end: it still continues in the external world. They are not really fighting against each other: it is the signal that we perceive in our eyes and in our heart until we can disconnect this electrical signal of perceiving in the mind, like moving into a whole new dimension of experience and live in the world of illusion.

Living in the world of illusion helps you to accept and practice everything that coexists. All things—good or bad—are in your mind and thoughts: you simply label them. You take it in and transcend it out to the external world. When you train your mind not to label things, that leads you towards realizing the opposite must allow coexistence. They are not fighting with each other. It happens to be the case that everything consists of positive and negative to make things easier for us, so that things can continue to develop and grow. If there were no negative, then the external world would have problems and cease to evolve, because no conscious creativity would be needed. So, it is not necessary to eliminate the opposite, but simply be vigilant and alert as its movement is fine. You must be aware that no matter how good and kind you are to everyone, you will still find someone on your horizon saying otherwise. Imagine that you struggle a lot with trying to get rid of certain things, but in a while it regroups again. You may have to let it go and open your mind and heart to that fact. As soon as you soften and have a more gentle approach to things and are open to accept whatever is occurring, then everything will just get better. You realize then that you do not need to fight anymore and everything is transform into the way you desire it to be. You do not translate things into good or evil anymore and let the world speak for itself. You begin get a fresh way of looking at things and become mindful, awake, kind and compassionate with your hopes and fears. We begin then to see clearly with less fear and less judgment. When this happens, the world we dwell in will translate for itself. You will begin to enjoy the world you live in very much. You think it is a peaceful and tranquil place, and you are living in a world of illusion. You now try to live with more curiosity than fear. It is the way to live in the world of illusion.

Chapter Six
The Power of Three

Crave this catchphrase in your mind: "The power of three sets you free." The three-fold experience is what you find pleasant or unpleasant that happened three times in a relevant short period of time. In other words, things happened to you, whether you recognized them as good or bad energy, three times, such as: envisioning that in a relevant short period of time a person won the lotto three times in a row. So, imagine that good fortune befalls him three times consecutively and say, "Oh! Well, God loves him."

On the other hand, imagine that you boil these three main poisonous herbs: fear, doubt and indecision. Preparing these three poisonous ingredients does not take long. In addition, things you crave, envy, greed and hatred, as well as the garden-variety aromatic plants of irritation go into the boiling pot. Making it pessimistically powerful, you add three further ingredients, aversion, aggression, and pain, plus three seeds, confusion, panic and suffering. Now, you have made a pot of the most poisonous and dangerous broth you can imagine. They are so dangerous, plus they multiply and grow without being observed. Now imagine the effect that this poison has in your life. It keeps you from seeing the world as it is, it makes you impaired, blind and out of touch to the extent that you won't recover overnight and it turns your life into turmoil and despair, so you suffer financial drawbacks and defeat. It is as if you were putting a band-aid over your wrist wounds. Until you are awakened and motivated, you will feel pain. You must address the problem properly and do not just throw the disc looking for chance and waiting to see how it falls.

If you want to eliminate these bad poisonous situations, then you must take steadfast action and do not allow these enemies to rob you and take you hostage by representing you. You need to liberate yourself, speak for yourself and represent yourself: do not let negativity control you. You need to clean these pessimistic thoughts out of your mind and stop being imprisoned by them and making your world less significant.

However, you may consider keeping these poisons, because, if you try to cast them out, then you miss the chance to trigger and reconnect with your Inner Being. It gives you an opportunity to awaken your Bodhichitta heart. When these poisons emerge, the shield that protects you within arises and transforms itself to become active. Your negative feelings are instantaneously shut off by the heart and replace angry, aggregative and unenthusiastic feelings with positive emotions. Without negativity in our minds, we never connect to endurance, compassion and kindness or open to fresh dimensions of our own Infinite being. You are able to contain any negativity and invite suffering, pain, or confusion to strengthen you.

It teaches you to reflect on that wound in your heart and either to act out or contain it. Use situations as an opportunity to feel your heart. Below all that jealousy, anger, dislike or misery about yourself, beneath all that depression, despair, and desperation, there's something tremendously soft that can lift you up, which is called Bodhichitta heart.

When bad things happen, gradually train your mind to learn not make it into a big deal. Begin to feel the wounded heart and soothe the anger. If someone comes along to try to harm you, it's pointless to stand there and let the person hurt you. It would be better to leave that situation and turn your attention to the fact that there is a wound in your heart, and you can always relate to that wound.

When you can do that, you have transformed anger and hatred into kindness and compassion and you forgive yourself for entering into that situation. If similar situations occur again, you would know how to contain and suppress it. It gives you a chance to change, to become more tolerant and patient and change your personality, temperament and the habit of dealing with any dilemma with calmness and tranquility. You turn the unwanted and undesired situations or circumstances into the path of contentment. You push yourself into awakening your Inner Soul and your ability to endure difficult situations is greater and you are open to forgiving and accepting others and yourself. You will always connect to your Inner Soul with the clarity of knowing when you face difficult situations, there is always a way out, and you can resolve it and extend your ability limitlessly.

Finally, people and situations in our lives are the main reasons for triggering our passions, endurance, kindness, or anger, aggression, and unawareness. It is like every morning you are addicted to having a cup of tea: that triggers your comfort and the positive things in life. If you can't get it, you feel something is missing. Other people could not care less about a cup of tea; it is not that important to them.

A lot of our thoughts are to do with something you like or an aversion, but if we can pay attention, we can always deal with the pleasant or unpleasant situation with a clear mind, without being blindfolded or making us feel very dumb. You should always stand up for yourself, speak for yourself and be yourself and let no others represent you. You control the horizontal and the vertical, and turn your attention to make steadfast action and transformations, and reconnect with your Inner Soul, your lucidity awakens your ability to see beyond.

Chapter Seven
From whence you begin

When you practice breathing exercises, taking breath in and sending it out is like making friends with yourself and particularly with your negative emotions. When you train your mind to crave positive energy in kindness and compassion, and at the same time accept the mess you are in, it is a reminder always to connect to your Inner Soul. Indeed, our thoughts can easily affect ourselves and others. Since we are interconnected in consciousness, whatever we think about can transcend into the atmosphere and affect the people around us and the world without. Now, we know how pollution and global warming affects the whole world. In fact, everything is interrelated, especially with ourselves, hence it is so important to love ourselves and be kind to ourselves. When we are kind to ourselves, we send kindhearted and caring energy and we crave positive emotions to the world so that the planet Earth can benefit.

Whatever you do, be kind to yourself, be gentle, be honest and do not be afraid to see your own image reflected in the mirror: that will affect how you respond and experience the world within and the world without. When you love yourself, you will love others, and when you love others, you will receive love back. However, when you train your mind to do good for others, it is uncertain what you will receive from others. You must simply follow what is within and transcend it to what is out there.

At any time, be conscious of your anger and react, and blaming others: it's really you who suffers. The people around you suffer and the atmosphere suffers as well because of the collective consciousness, but you suffer the most because you are being observed by all the negative energy suppressed within, causing you to feel aversion to yourself.

You respond because, unreasonably, you think it will release some of your anger that you have suppressed within and that would make you feel better. We have to do this because it helps to release whatever restrains us within and transcend it to the emptiness and let it dissolve into air so that our anger is expressed, and we no longer bear the weight on our shoulders. You possess the power to liberate yourself in consciousness and achieve the moment of gratification by releasing the unwanted desires and attitudes from your life. Similarly, it applies to joy and happiness. Often, when you feel happy, your joyful expression will be shown on your face and it will release joy from within and send it out to the external world.

However, if you cannot eradicate your aggregative moments, then the nightmare remains. You tell whoever is near you to get out of your way: you might feel calmness and tranquility within for a short while, but the problem remains unsolved and anger extends and ultimately it hurts you more. It is as if you work out for an hour to release your excessive energy, for then you feel good. But, in the present moment, it looks as if you shut off everything, and continue to be hurt within.

Now, if you change your mind and surrender yourself and accept the mess you have made is nobody's fault and believe the adverse situations will pass and commit to allowing yourself to make life transformations—then you reconnect and touch the soft spot of the Bodhictitta's heart: it eases all your hard feelings. You awaken to love and care for yourself, and gradually you become more benevolent and empathetic to others. You crave love and compassion, you speak better words and give blessings to whoever you meet on a daily basis. This stimulus occurs if you do it properly: surely, it will benefit others and the world. So, the point is that indeed we are consciously connected. What you do to others, you apply to yourself. Then, what you do to yourself, you transcend to others. It is the cause and effect that brings back everything to the creator, so that he will have a chance to taste what he had done to others is like. If it is a good deed, surely he will receive many blessings and a fruitful return, while the opposite is that he is guaranteed a chance to be burned.

You begin where you make transformations in your life. This is very important for to allow the change to take place. You start from whence you came. You do not start in the middle, but right at the spot where you want to begin. You do not need to wait for the right moment because any moment is the appropriate moment to make a transformation in your life. The good thing about this meditation practice is that there is no requirement. It is about changing you and making you feel good and fresh after you have done it.

Before you begin this practice perhaps you may be the most hated person in the world or maybe you are the most greedy and jealous person on the horizon. You think you are one of the kind of people who hates themselves. You may be thinking you are a lonely person who dwells on this lonely planet. All this gives you a genuine good reason to start practicing meditation to change.

Now you may start by taking your breath in and out and gradually, letting the unwanted thoughts go, not trying to contain them, thoughts that are full of hatred, jealousy, greed, and being unloved, thoughts that contain lacks: whatever they might be, just eliminate them all. You can perceive as you continue thinking and eliminating them that ultimately your mind is empty. Your mind has no thought and the empty mind contains thoughtlessness and it cannot hurt you anymore. You start to feel more energy, in your neck, your head, and the whole body is fresh and rejuvenated with positive vibrations and emotions. You now know your life is worth continuing and you no longer feel the suppression within that put you under pressure: in that moment, all translates to the wealth of who you really are. You have just turned your ignorance, anguish, aversion, doubt, and illusions of fear and indecision to becoming more active, passionate, kind, and a loving and caring person. Thanks to the negative poisonous herbs and other ingredients, your entire pessimistic attitude is now a suspended shield and is contained by kindness, compassion and openness of heart—no further transformation is needed. Now, you realize that letting it go is the key to connecting your wealth and happiness within to that which you already have. All the trouble in you is eradicated in the now. You activate the Inner Soul in the now from right when you begin. No matter where you are, or what you are doing, you should never forget to practice meditation. It changes what is around you and the world benefits from you through collective consciousness as we are all one.

One evening you were tired and so you turned in and

dreamed this scenario: you find your home was dominated by and filled with uninvited strangers. They were cooking your food, using your computer, reading your books and watching your television and using everything you have in your home. The thing is, you don't know how to kick them out of your home. Even though you were aware they were just an illusion projected in your brain that is in your mind—the unwanted part of yourself—yet you did not know how to deal with them.

So you thought they were a hologram and unreal, so it would be very easy to banish them. You gathered them together: you thought you taught them compassion, kindness and openness, and emptiness. You mentioned that they are your negative emotions and help to balance your energy in your physical body. It triggered your Inner Heart to become activate to protect you from further negatives, but things became beyond your control. But, there was no respond from the unwanted guests. You thought you were helpless and nobody was going to leave and you were not leaving and nor were they. Finally, you said to the strangers, "We are not going anywhere, let's live well together". As that was said, all the strangers disappeared. But, one stranger remained there who did not leave. That is the old belief that you have held for years from your heritage and so you find it difficult to get rid of—its force of resistance is greater than you and it refuses to leave your comfortable home. You thought that at least you tried, but failed. Ultimately, you surrender to what it is and let go. Then, the stranger leaves. When the force vanishes, so do the negative emotions.

The strangers have gone from your home because you gave in and no longer forced anything to happen: then everything began to fall into place. You became more relaxed to the situations and circumstances and even people in your lives: if they have left you, let them go and do not feel sorry you lost them. It applies to every acquisition that we have accumulated, as detachment will benefit us from having further desires. Then, everything will emerge and you will not need to struggle and fight for it. It comes to you automatically, effortlessly and easily without further ado.

When you experience adversity in your life, you practice detachment and non-resistance and mere taking-in. You surrender yourself, you aware who you are, and acknowledge and love yourself. When undesired feelings and emotions occur, you take it all in and transcending it out to the Universe and connect with how other people feel. When energy returns, it will actually make you feel better because it develops a relationship with others who feel the same pain as you, and you see that you are not living alone in a lonely planet. It proves again that it genuinely awakens our relationships with all people through consciousness. We are all citizens of the world and can easily be connected and united through consciousness, becoming one conscious thought. In fact, all living things are interconnected, not just human beings. All healing energy comes from the Universal Source through the hands of a healer in human form in the physical world.

When you connect with the pain within, you can find a loophole of space in which you can awaken the emptiness of Bodhichitta's heart. You begin to connect that loophole when you relate directly with your problems: you are completely breaking the ego-self.

When we begin to accept the pain, it opens our hearts to what's undesired and unwanted. When we relate directly in this way with boldness to face the unwanted areas of our lives, the breathing spaces for the ego begin to be freshen. By the same token, when we open our genuine hearts and make them glow and share all positive things with others, that completely undoes the opinion of the ego, it reverses the suffering. It overcomes the crisis to give peace and rise beyond pain to pleasure. Whether you are giving in or sending it out, you are opening an inner vast reserve and this spiritual awakening connects with the soft spot of Bodhichitta's heart and a shift in perception is all it takes to attract spiritual happiness and live in the imagination and the illusion of the material richness of the physical world.

So now try this practice. Find a comfortable place to sit down. The connection with Bodhichitta is quick and flashes to you naturally. Close your eyes. Relax your whole body and take in and send out and begin to visualize all the negative energy and emotions you have towards anything: begin to gather them and slowly flow them out of your body. You perceive there is a black ball flashing up from your feet and hands, through your arms and legs, up through your body and neck and it begins to gather this negative energy into one focal point; then you breath out with purple light. You are breathing in with suffering and pain, experiencing the texture of anger or feelings of lack and envy. That is actually what you have hidden within and it pervades you and is in the mind during the quiet session of meditation; you experience all in openness. Then, you convert these painful experiences and substitute them with the Divine light flowing through your whole body and force the negative out by breathing in and out until you satisfy all negativity in the mind and body. You are emptying all negativity from your body and mind.

Now, you continue to focus upon specific heartfelt objects of suffering. You visualize the pain of a specific person you wish that you could help. You transcend out positive emotions and energy to lessen his/her pain at the moment. This can be craved to any person that you met or passes by you in the street, or yourself and the pain you are feeling in the now. The point is sending positive energy to anyone reduces suffering and pain, even though it is unavoidable and real. However, we must do it with kindness, compassion and openness to attain the effect of genuinely helping to clean and lighten the weight of Universal suffering of all (that also includes animals and trees in the world of illusion). You are working on extending the ease of suffering to *all* and you make it real, like a hologram, and vivid. On the other hand, it gives you an opportunity to work with other people in the world to strengthen and power up the healing energy and hopefully it lessens the suffering quicker so that it becomes possible that everyone can achieve peace instead of pain and sorrow and overcome hatred, jealousy and greed and detach themselves from the desire of wanting and avoid fighting each other and accept the reality of who we are: that we are intellectual infinite beings, interrelated with one another including animals and plants. Therefore, one person's suffering will affect all people in the world, because we all come from the same place. So, beginning now, we use our innate abilities to create something that is of benefit to all with one purpose in mind: to work with anyone else and transcend the light energy to lighten the suffering in the world.

Sometimes when you look at this world, it is full of murder, war, and disharmony with one another. When you look at these problems, you feel negative emotions, and then you do not feel positive. Hence, you must work with your Inner Being and clean your inner consciousness. You must clean away your anxiety, anger, and range first, then you can transcend out positive energy to others. Through your positive attention and attitude, you assist others to attain what they have been missing in their lives, so they know what they want through the echo of attracting what is important to them in that moment. When you focus upon their well-being and recovery from a lack, you actually connect to your own Inner Soul and see them well: you have the chance to help them make an improvement in their lives through you and your soul. By doing so, you develop your sympathy for others and begin to understand that you can help and influence people's surroundings through consciousness. You also see your own pain through a mirror of other pains. Your heart evolves more and more: even if someone has insulted you, you still stay calm and tranquil because you understand where everybody's coming from. You simply take in the whole situation and send out positive energy. You transcend your own pain and you use your own pain to understand that suffering is Universal, shared by everyone. You constantly practice taking in and sending out relief to yourself and push for something that activates your Inner Soul. You let your experiences extend to other parts of the globe and they gradually extend to help everyone and benefit all.

Chapter Eight

Enlightenment—achievement of a spiritual state

Enlightenment means you utilize undesired, unwanted, and unfavorable situations and circumstances in your life and transform them into profound material wealth and abundance and radiant joy and unshakable peace in your life. Ultimately, it brings an end to suffering and an awakening or resurrection. You must understand that enlightenment does not mean "zero suffering." When you are desireless and detached from want and willing to offer and share your wealth with everybody, then you are aware that your true nature is infinite: you can have more of everything, and your mind is emptied and not tempted by the ego. Finally, you have come to a sense of mental and physical touch in the present and are conscious of your surroundings: that is enlightenment.

Enlightenment is an awakened body, mind and spirit in one, as well as a connection with the external state. Therefore, you are at peace within and without. It not only suffering brings to an end as well as instant conflicts felt within and without, but it also ceases unwanted thinking and silences the mind. Your mind is stillness, emptied, and actually you free the mind and immediately connect to a higher consciousness, which is more powerful than your thoughts or just thought. It connects you with the true beauty of peace, love and harmony to transcend beyond the mind. Therefore, it cannot bring any vulnerable thought to you to make you suffer from the illusions of fear, doubt, and indecision. You connect your emotional thoughts with your Inner Soul and transform them into one mind and one soul. Hence, you walk on the path of inner serenity and tranquility and things go well and make you feel good. It is as though you enjoy the beauty of snow falling outside your window and the reflection of the light off the floor. You appreciate the nature that brings this effect, so you can enjoy and feel delighted.

So, what is enlightenment? Enlightenment is just a normal name saying that all of a sudden you have understood that you do not need to fight, to struggle, to defend or explain further what you do or why you do it: you let things speak and translate for themselves. You do not need the approval or acceptance of others, but you rise above that horizon and people will know your aptitudes. Then, everything will shift with confidence and you just are. You have awakened to who you really are and things will happen naturally and effortlessly. There is no good or bad in this world of illusion. An opposite always exists: good and evil are there all the time and suffering and pain are what this world is about. If there were no suffering, then we would not know what sorrow is: when catastrophe arose it would be difficult for us to deal with it. It is almost impossible feel no pain in life because things are ever-changing, ever-evolving in an ever-lasting eternity and it all changes moment by moment. We want things to work out of their own accord; we want to know "about me or my success" and cling on the ego of "me-winning." When you do not win, you feel like you have let yourself down and disappointed others. You feel categorized as a loser. But, when you are aware and accept that there are always challengers on the horizon to challenge you, better and more intelligence than you, then that is your enlightenment. You no longer feel bad and do not need to try to push thing to suit you. The more fear you have within, the more your aptitude grows. Rather, choose to relax, lower your expectations and pride and go with the flow. When you do go out, you find the experience more and more settling and agreeable. You become in touch with the world and nature and your heart, and are less fearful and less irritable. You feel a sense of self-awareness and a powerful sense of awakening in the now. You attain a certain degree of inner peace and calmness that you feel within: that is the self-awareness of enlightenment.

Each time you want to do something you do not need to agree with your mind, but just listen to your Inner Self, every time you do that, the Bodhichitta's heart lights up and your consciousness grows stronger and possesses more strength. You will catch yourself smiling by listening to the heart instead of the mind. This means that you are no longer controlled by the ego, since your Inner Soul does not depend on it. You should also pay attention to the recurring thinking that comes to you from nowhere. You may find it helpful to listen to the message. It comes from the Inner Self and must have significance in your current situation. It brings a sense of your own presence; it is not a thought. It arises beyond the mind, and from the inner consciousness of the compassionate heart. The message is worth paying attention to. It alerts you to be awake in its presence and fully present in the now. You do better in its presence since all things are available to you in your consciousness and created in the creative consciousness.

Hence, you experience everything and unlock the portal of your innate power in consciousness. Now, you begin to develop your feelings in the now. You practice compassion, kindness and a connection with the Inner Heart. You begin to see what happens when you do not relate your problems in the moment: it brings fear in the now. It also vibrates many undesired and unwanted memories forward to the present, making you feel you are being locked in a small room with the windows closed. You feel a shortness of breath and you are breathing in fear, anger, anxiety, loneliness and helplessness. However, since you have triggered the Inner Power, you are able to contain and release the tender, shaky, fearful feelings in your own heart and, therefore, you are no longer frightened by those feelings when the problems arise again.

When you practice in this way, you are truthful about your own feelings and you begin to create a sense of understanding of the feelings of other people and the world. You could feel in some parts of the world that people are being laughed at because of their color, race, and customs. You realize that, throughout time people, have found themselves in humiliating situations because they are weaker than other people surrounding them. This helps to open your heart to others and feel their pain in a way you had not done before, but now you share their experiences.

This is where you feel a sense of gratitude and appreciation of your life coming from. You feel connected to them for their boldness against all unfairness and handling great difficulties through facing pain and sorrowful situations and converting them into the path of consciousness. We will never feel perfect and we continue to face life with challenges and feel insufficient, but we can use these experiences to awaken our hearts and consciousness and carry on our journey to the end. We can just be and always act as who we really are: we do not need to please others in order to justify our abilities in handling things. Do not let others confuse your aptitudes: you must have confidence and trust in yourself. But, whatever your style, you should never keep the "I or me" attitude: if you do, then you will fail. However, you need to keep trying no matter what: in any situation or circumstance you will never fail, and when the right moment approaches, your efforts will pay off and you will gain success in your life. You will see a rainbow at the end of the tunnel: that is enlightenment. You have awakened to what you want to see in your life: the life you want to preserve and encourage others to live life fearlessly and bravely. We should always compliment painful and joyful experiences, since they bring vivid color into our lives, so that we can embrace life more instead of condemn life. We need to accept that life contains suffering, yet believe we can overcome suffering, and substitute it for a lucid mind and peaceful heart. Ultimately, feeling good within will bring more kindness, openness, compassion and love to be transcended and stirred into the air and sent out to everyone so that people and nature, and the whole world will benefit. It is an awakening of heart that helps us to bring a peaceful end across the globe, with one purpose: to bring peace and benefits to all.

Chapter Nine
Convert and condemn it

In the physical world, we like to blame others for our own blunders and sometimes even cover them up so that no one knows about them. The quick response of human nature is to condemn others for their faults and consider that they are always right. We think that to blame others can help us to escape from our own conscience of faults. It is true that in every part of the world the blaming game operates instead of the truth. That is why we face war after war continuously across the globe. We must see that blaming others just does not work. We cannot accept others' differences: therefore, we fight each other, killing, murdering, raping and using our own bodies as bombs to kill others with one purpose, to destroy. Unfortunately, this is our world we see today. The truth is perceived everywhere and hardly anyone can find any peace in the world. A blaming game, greed and envy happen in every corner of the world and is the naked truth.

But what do people really want in their lives? They can easily give you steadfast answers: they just want to be happy and free from stress and fear. When we perceive the world this way, no one is willing to look into their hearts to dissolve the troubles and chaos through peaceful means and they believe that blaming others is the only way. We are wearing a veil and do not show our real selves, we hide what we are thinking in our minds. Our words and thoughts are not in alignment with our actions. In other words, a person can promise you everything by just sweet-talking. He knew in his mind he faked it. When he meets you again he regards it as though nothing happened. You do not know whether he has forgotten his word, or simply gave an empty promise and the promise was never created in his own mind. In this situation, we need to reflect our own fault as well. You should not blame him, but begin to accept that you have made a mistake by allowing and driving yourself to enter into the undesired situation with this person. Now, you look at the problem and make changes yourself. You ensure you will never enter into any trusting relationship with that person again. As soon as you start making transformations in yourself, you guide yourself instead of pushing things away, you begin to be in touch with reality and realize that the Inner Heart is the most trusted source yon can cling onto for assistance. When you prepare for everything and lighten up and align with the soft spot then things will transform to your pleasure. The point is that you must trust your own aptitudes and insight and never underestimate your own capability of resolving problems and so loose the command to others. Ultimately, you can win; you feel good within and trust your Inner Heart that guides you to walk on the right path: you will never need to cling on other people's faith. It would be a huge blunder to do so. If you follow your Inner Consciousness you will never fail. You will always find joy, happiness, peace and success.

Can we put the blame into one basket, take it in and accept

it as our own? Can we hold the feelings of anger, feel the blame, and feel the helplessness and treat it with compassion and kindness and loveliness by using the practice of breathing in and transcending it out with gentleness and benevolence? Can we fill and stir the air with the calmness and peace we crave for ourselves? You see it is wrong to condemn and blame others rather than accepting it as your own fault for driving yourself into the dilemma and condemning it without being able to withdraw from the circumstances. You need to clean the mind and stop contemplating and conveying to yourself that you allowed it: leave what is wrong and what is right alone and let everything go, transcend it to the Universal Source for that matter and let the Universe be your judge and carry on your life.

You may find it difficult to blame yourself for the blunders because it is really somebody's fault that caused the adverse situation and surroundings; however, if you can take the heat and accept the mistakes and drop the emotions of feeling that you are being treated unfairly or lied to, then you attain inner peace and tranquility and a sense of release from the unwanted desires of anger, hatred and aversion towards the subject matter that had driven your energy. In fact, when you continuously focus upon the subject matter with anger and aversion, you have given your energy away, and you suffer most from it, and the person also suffer, and the surroundings are also affected by your negative emotions. So, it is worth abandoning it and replacing it with positive energy: cheer up and crave your life with peace and love and own the feelings yourself instead of blaming others.

You find it improper to transfer all blame to yourself because the ego only cares for "I and me." As you continue to make changes, the solid ground of the ego-concept is broken down and is airless. It is not going to regroup concerning "I or me" or

"I am suffering": because of that, therefore, "I am angry." These self-talk negative emotions to yourself are substituted by energy from where the mind and body meet and you begin to understand it is for your own benefit not to blame others but allow and accept it as the beginning of a positive relationship with yourself: get the Me to begin to cheer up, and cooperate with your Inner Heart and your mood will stop wavering. At the same time, lighten up your consciousness and be aware of the environment and, ultimately, feel the transformation of the silence, the powerful energy of its presence, and attain the degree of real peace that you feel within.

When people fool you with empty promises and you feel that you are being fooled by them, if you are not afraid of being a fool, that transforms the major point of standing up for yourself and being yourself and accepting that people can only fool you once. That unloads the burden from your shoulders and immediately triggers the Inner Heart and you ground yourself and let the situation fade away. The point is, do not be afraid of being fooled by others, but always prepare yourself and see it rise on the horizon so that you know your life is always navigated by yourself, but not cling onto others. Do not be frightened: dive deep into the Inner Self and see what creates your frustration and anger: eradicate and substitute it with compassion and kindness and stir it into the air by breathing out and feeling the energy within and without. At the same time, you will weaken the cling of the ego, and your kindness and compassion will arise. Again, we may be deceived, but we do not need to be ashamed of being fooled by others: contain and treat the obstacles with kindness and loveliness and turn them around and continue to love yourself and be bold.

Chapter Ten

Eliminate the pain in the Consciousness

A great amount of our pain is avoidable and unnecessary. It is self-created, as long as you allow the mind command over your life.

The pain that you possess is real, but normally comes in the form of denial, in a sense of resistance to the truth. Your response to your pain is contained within negative emotions. In the phase of thought, the resistance is some form of opinion. The strength of the pain depends on the degree of your resistance to the now: this converts to how strongly you are recognized by your mind. The mind always has an aversion to the present moment and tries to escape from it. The *more* you *agree* with the *mind*, the *more* you *suffer*. On the other hand, the more you dwell in the now, the less pain you feel or you are free from suffering: you are free of the egoistic mind.

The resistance of the mind is always an aversion to the present moment because it cannot operate without time, both the past and the future, so it sees an eternity now as frightening. In fact, time and mind are undetectable.

In our world everything works according to a time sequence; for instance, I have a project due at 3 pm or I have Doctor's appointment at 3 pm today. The Space Shuttle will liftoff at precisely 23.00 hours. What time is now? The time is now. What else would it be?

Indeed, everyone agrees with you: we need the mind and time to function, making everything possible in our world. We get to the point that our lives are controlled in reality and that is where ennui sets in and causes us pain and suffering.

The ego's mind always likes to be in command and ensure that it continuously hides the now with the past and it brings something to you that has not yet occurred. The past and the fluid future have time sequences that exist only in the mind, but you are an Infinite Being: everything you create or recreate is happened in this moment in creative consciousness, not later. The mind has hidden the now from you; therefore, you always think of the past or the unfolding future, which is an increasingly heavy weight of time sequences that concern our minds. Everyone is suffering under the time sequences, whenever we have to add time to every moment or deny the present is the most precious moment so we keep looking into the fluid future, which has not yet been conceived but only exists in the mind; it only an illusion and never a reality. Our mind also holds a vast amount of enduring pain, which has been collected through memories accumulated over time, due to things that occurred in the past.

If you no longer wish to create this pain, then stop living in the past or use thoughts from the past as rarely as possible and face the actual aspects of your life. Stop contemplating the past. Begin to dwell in the present moment and believe the present is all you need to focus upon and transform becoming into your primary focus. You are aware of the present moment and you utilized the now before and now is the time to apply it more and pay less attention to the unreal past, which has no merit in any pillar of your life. So, why are you dwelling in a place where there is no actual benefit to you, but only brings chaos, despair and painful and hurtful emotions to your life? It would be unwise if you do not use something already created for you, which is more fruitful and more abundant than to create and manifest something you resist from within and know brings that which can hurt you. What would be more ridiculous than to oppose life itself and the conscious moment that is and will be always in consciousness? Detach from whatever has happened that you can never regain, and begin living in consciousness, and see life transform and work well for you instead of resisting you. Never allow doubt in your mind and always live in the creative consciousness in the power of Now.

You can always observe that the mind likes to judge, create pain and suffering and vulnerability for you, especially when your life is not in good shape and the mind continues to bring you more worries and fears. However, when you step out of fear, worry and doubt and the resistant powers, you can then transform the present moment so it is dynamic. This will give you a chance to perceive your life is dynamic in the Now and take action in the creative consciousness if needs be.

Whatever the present moment offers you, simply accept it and seize any opportunity that is open to you in the Now and accept it as if you had already chosen it. Always work with it in the moment and never against it. Make friends with the present moment and begin to see miracles happen to you. This will miraculously transmute the four areas of your life.

When you are unable to access the present moment, immediately you notice the emotional pain that you had experienced returning again. It blends with fear, worry and doubt from the past so that it begins to take over your mind and physical body. This bad memory goes back as deep as your childhood, it is one that you do not want to know, it was caused by the unconsciousness of the world into which you were born.

This emotional pain can occur in two scenarios: it happens to a deeply unhappy person. This person's entire life is full of painful and hurtful experience. While in other situations, a person may suffer partial pain due to involvement with whole or partial situations linked to past loss, being scammed by people or by emotional hurt. All these painful experiences can easily be triggered by consciously resonating with the past. Since it is already half awakened from its inactive stage, even a mere thought by you can fully activate it.

Some physical pains are less dreadful and less important, but some are destructive and harsh. Because of the physical pains in their bodies, some even turn violent to other people. It becomes more difficult for their emotions and feelings, as it is deeply negative and contains as many self-destructive thoughts as possible: it leads people to commit suicide because of their physical bodily pains.

If you thought you knew yourself, well then, think again! It may not be so until you confront the creature that dwells in your mental home for the first time: you will probably be shocked by what you find out. However, it is important for you to observe and be vigilant in yourself so that you are aware of it. Vigilance for any sign that may activate your undesired physical bodily pain is necessary. This may be in the form of impatience, anger, stress, depression, wavering, moodiness, poor relationships, and the like. Pay attention to any sign and attempt to catch it the moment it is about to awaken from its sleeping stage.

Your pained body wants to get out of the pain as much as you do. But, you need to identify with it and then deal with it. Then, you will be able to become you again. You need to feed your body with good food so it can continue to survive living through you. Anything that you create consumes energy such as joy and happiness, anger, hatred, grief, negative emotions, violence and influence from the external environment and even illness. The pain energy will create a situation in your life that reflects back its own energy for it to live on you. Pain and suffering can only feed on pain energy and it can never feed on joy and happiness. They are on different paths and have an aversion to each together like water and oil and so will never mix. They will never blend in actuality.

One of the most serious drawbacks of suffering in life is loneliness. Perhaps a painful experience pops into your mind that you do not really want to contemplate. However, you have to cope with and face it, especially when you enter the pain of illness. It creates a form of emotional drama, inner sadness and grief that the mind perceives. Anything can trigger the weakened mind to think of many negative and unrealistic pictures, yet you have forgotten the life that is given to you can handle any situation on its own.

When you keep contemplating the unwanted and disturbing image, it strengthens its presence and power to irritate you further. Your heartbeat and breathing is faster than normal. In fact, you have perceived this terrible sense of horror and projected it to the external world. More of these pains continuously emerge in your mind and you become a victim of your own pain and suffering. You are not conscious of which were caused by the negative emotions perceived within and which ones came from what you saw in external conditions: you wish you had someone with you that can understand it. However, it is your continuous thought, perception and behavior that you design by making yourself miserable: this keeps the pain going. If you were truly conscious of this lonely feeling, you could dissolve it by telling yourself that you are fine, you can handle any situation in consciousness with a lucid mind. You believe you have been given life to handle any situation by yourself. You know when you change your mind, it transforms everything.

The way out of a pain-driven life is to focus pain and suffering on love. To achieve this goal, we need to direct our minds to become more careful, so that we can catch our pessimistic thoughts before they are fully manifested into our reality.

Although you do not continue to energize your pain through recognition, however, a certain momentum must be met, and is not like a spinning wheel that will turn and, when turning, hopefully it will stop in the right spot and no longer be parallel to your pain. Under the circumstances, it may create a new ache in a different part of your body, but it won't stay. However, as long as you stay in consciousness with a lucid mind, eventually the pain will go away. You will regain inner peace and tranquility from your Bodhichitta heart. The compassion and kindness in your heart kicks in, but you must be present to observe and be vigilant of the physical pain directly and feel its energy. You can control your thinking with the help of inner realization. This hot spot forms a silent shield redirecting your thoughts from pessimistic emotions and feelings so that it silently reminds you that you are not thinking thoughts of kindness, but are under the control of the egoistic thoughts: as soon as you realize, "I am alone, I am in pain, I am angry" you begin somehow to be breathless and become airless. The hot spot pulls you out of the negative thought field and returns you to the positive energy thought field: it closes that door you do not need which offers you no protection in consciousness. The moment your thinking ceases to be in alignment with the negative emotional energy field of your bodily pain, you identify with it and automatically cease from feeding it with your thoughts. The negative thoughts drop away and you simply let go of the conditions and circumstances you do not need and you begin to feel good with inner stillness and silence. You return to your true self again in the consciousness.

You must set aside everything so that you have a lucid mind with nothing in it when the mind is purified and consumed by nothingness and emptied. Then your mind is returned to point zero, so that subsequently you connect back to the void, the emptiness, and are united with the Universal Source: that is where you originated as a pure soul, an infinite being.

So, you purify your mind and observe whatever you feel within, rather than defending or trying to use strengths and skills to fight with your challenger when often you realize that you could not thrive. However, when you apply less effort, without resistant and dissolving the mind in consciousness, then you achieve the results you want that will allow you to accomplish what you want effortlessly and effectively. In other words, you no longer fight with your past pains and quickly all pains fade away.

Once you have understood the practice of non-resistance in the present and allow things to go through by observing what happens within you, you recognize it by experiencing it in consciousness: then you have obtained, to your own advantage, the most powerful tool of transformation.

This is not to deny pain and suffering in your physical body. You may still have to live with that until the pains are healed. This is especially so when you live most of your adulthood with emotional pain but have never dealt with it or recognized it. You have created an unhappy life for your pained body and believe in your mind that you could not make any transformation because of who you are. In that case, the misconception of the identification of who-you-really-are is misunderstood through the power of fear and illusion. In fact, it is you who allowed the pain to continue in your physical body with your strong beliefs and resistance so that you could not change, or you have never attempted to make any transformation and accept the pain. You are risking your whole life being one of suffering pain for some unconscious reason and you risk your life continuously becoming one of the fearful unhappy self.

You are in possession of your own life and you can pass through any situation and circumstance. You have never attempted to release the pain in your physical body, but rather you endorse more pains and are continuously flogging yourself with the whip. The inside of you resists your actions with all its power and tries to connect with you and warn you. But, you never listen to the silent voice and you relax your mind to negative thinking: you should stop pulling on the tether and the ever-ready whip.

Gradually you are getting into harness and listen to the silence within yourself. Vigilance is the attachment to your physical pain. Be very vigilant. Observe the strange pleasure you gain from being unhappy. You begin to watch and observe the compulsion to think and speak about it. You realize the resistance ceases once you recognize you are now dwelling in creative consciousness in the now. Then, you can take your attention regarding your pain, stay in the present as the witness, and begin making a conscious transformation.

After long periods of training, your mind and you begin to face round and believe it is time to accept the inner spirit, and the pull of the ungoverned painful life is finally broken and you turn to become gentler. But, the mind has not yet given you full confidence. You still contemplate the negative thoughts: in a while you drop them completely because you are aware that the pain no longer exists: it is only an illusion created by the mind. You know your physical pain is healed, as it is unimpeded by the consciousness. With no fear and no doubt, the pained body is now restored to health and you genuinely relax in peace and enjoy an overflowing life.

You are in the here and now: however, the mind is in the fluid future making you lose touch with the power of the now. This creates a constant gap of anxiety. If you can identify with your mind, that anxiety gap will benefit you constantly. You know you can cope with the present and dwell in the moment, but you cannot cope with something that is projected by the egoistic mind that you cannot endure.

Furthermore, you need to recognize with the mind that the ego is controlling your life because of fear and the unknown future and this is due to your vulnerable and emotional nature feeling insecure and seeing yourself under a constant threat or danger. On the outside, the ego may show itself as confident. It is the emotion of the body's reaction to your mind. The body continuously receives a false emotional signal and reaction from the ego. Consequently, danger and fear is the message that your body constantly generated.

Fear has many faces and can be generated by many causes. Fear of death, fear of illness, fear of being harmed, fear of scarcity, and reasons can be created instantaneously by the conditions that are around you. To the gloomy mind, death could happen instantly. In the egoistic mind, fear of death affects every corner of your life. A simple illness can easily ignite thoughts of normal things becoming many threatening diseases that could occur to you. It is difficult to have a clear mind, especially when you are sick and cannot clearly identify the current situation which brings in many negative emotional thoughts that are unnecessary, and that this is due to a fear of death. So, because of the egoistic mind, you refuse to accept you are wrong. The mind's sense of self identification is gravely threatened by total destruction. Consequently, you, as the ego, cannot afford to be wrong. Being wrong is to be eliminated. It is like fighting a war: if you fail, then you die.

Once you have recognized the egoistic mind, you are set free to pursue your own pleasures: whether they are right or wrong makes no difference to your sense of self, so the deeply unconscious need to be right, which is a form of distress, will no longer exist. You wend your way homeward while your mind quietly follows. The mind and the self are now surrounded by calmness and peace; you are perfectly at ease and carefree, and so is your mind. The thoughts that penetrate the mind are calm and lucid, without negative influences and emotions. The ego mind is now following your direction and movements without complaint. Nowhere can the ego mind be seen and you are the master of the mind. This is the end of power games, which built the relationship with the mind. Your resistant power over things is weakened and non-resistance is strength. True power is attained within and it is inevitably yours in the present.

So, when you have recognized your ego mind and constantly connect with the power within your true self, you will have no fear, as fear is no longer your constant companion. On the other hand, when you identify with your mind and disconnect from the deeper self of the rooted Infinite Being, you will have fear as your friend. Some people are living with constant fear, with mood fluctuations and their mind is not at ease as they have a sense of being under a distant threat from others. Most people do not realize they are in bed with the greater power of all evil—the ultimate dynamic energy of fear.

However, when the Ego mind is tamed, then the Infinite Mind is activated and becomes very active and nothing remains unresolved: all is completed and this is the way it should be without the interference of the Ego mind. When the finite ego mind and the Infinite Being are mixed together, that is enlightenment. The mind is reconnected and returned to nothingness where the void, emptiness, purity, and the Universal Source are found, becoming one power.

When you experience nothing in the consciousness then nothing is really omitted, but you still have the transformative power of peace within.

It is difficult to believe that our lives in the physical world are led by the ego: as a result, your life is not at genuine ease. So, you cannot be at peace with life and fulfill anything you want, except that occasionally you get what you wanted when creative thoughts have just been fulfilled. The ego is a self-center egoistic mind that always likes to win and it needs to be satisfied instantly. The most common recognitions of the ego are accumulated acquisitions, social status, political power, knowledge, wealth, physical appearance, outstanding aptitude, personal achievement; there are also many other attributes that the ego wants you to attain, but none of these attributes can define the real you.

Do you find this acceptable or ridiculous? Some of us may find it all right to possess all these attributes and there is nothing to be frightened of. This is because the matter is that, sooner or later, you want to accumulate them all and this is led by the ego. You want to be a very successful person on Earth. But, unknown to you, all of these possessions will have to be relinquished when you leave the world. Then you think of your true Being, and this does not need any of those aspects to gratify its Infinite Self. The Infinite Mind does not need any of those things to satisfy its wants and needs. The Infinite has no scarcity, yet embraces everything. Through the combination of the finite and infinite, we express and experience everything in the material world. The Infinite is the true power, but the power of craving thought from the activity of the conscious mind makes us believe that action brings results in the physical world and converts them into material desire. But, when one feels death is near, this will strip away all of your needs and wants, because you know it is time to let go and everything will return to emptiness. In fact, death occurs only in the physical body in the illusion of the physical world: the infinite is never-ending for eternity. Therefore, no death ever occurs.

Chapter Eleven
Be Thankful to All

Showing gratitude to everyone is an aspect of truly loving and making peace with ourselves and that we rejected ourselves unconsciously. Through doing so, we also make peace with people we are not in tune with. When you are surrounded by people you are not in tune with, it always gives you a chance to practice love yourself, to tame and improve your temperament, and be grateful to all.

Now, think of people you dislike—people who are short tempered, threatening, contemptuous, wavering, angry, greedy, envious and jealous—now think that a lot of these features are familiar, but we simply cannot face them. These pessimistic qualities dwell latent within us, silently. However, we may, in harness, accept these negative descriptions of our own by default, which are unconsciously projected onto the external world. People who repel us reflect in us the features that we find unacceptable that we cannot realize and see. It is as though these people triggered a cause and effect we have not yet identified. Before we want to criticize others, we must remind ourselves of our own qualities. In other words, they are a reflection of our own shadows, that mirror and reflect us, as we carry them around all the time.

People who emerged in our lives—whether they came in a flash or entered on our path—have reasons for being there. Their emergence or interference in our lives is perhaps only for a short interval, but it reminds us to learn from them or any situation, especially when we are in consciousness. The people and events remind us to catch sight of our own mischief through the observation of others. We are hiding in a secret room with a veil on and we watch every movement of others, and at the same time we appreciate that it looks familiar because the reflection of others reflects and alerts us. Then we know to appreciate people to awaken us to learn from it and make a transformation in our attitudes and eliminate the phobias in our wakened hours.

You have the aptitude to learn from everything; you have the innate ability, wisdom, knowledge and kindness. Therefore, if conditions allow and support you, and you are bold enough to open your mind, you will find yourself opening up to the knowledge, wisdom and compassion that you learn and observe in the secret room. It is like drumming into your own Source and you realize what you already possess. Your willingness opens your mind, your heart and your eyes, to allow the circumstances of your life to become your guide. With consciousness in the here and now, you will be able to realize for yourself the roots of despair and what triggers joy and happiness.

"Be grateful to all" means to be awakened so that we know that we must change our attitude, not put on a veil, not be unaware that we are hurting ourselves and see something inside the bubble of protection, when we do not perceive the whole thing clearly.

"Be grateful to all" means that you should let conditions and mistakes be your guide and usually the toughest ones teach you the best. There are people in your life that help you to learn, make you think, repent, and keep you dynamic. They won't leave you: your parents, your lover, your family, your children, your friends and your acquaintances that you see daily, and they are a part of the situation you cannot avoid.

Every situation teaches you something because there are no immediate solutions to the problem. Did someone ever strike out at you for no apparent reason, leaving you hurt, angry and confused by such behavior? Most likely your initial reaction was to strike back, but if you were able to distance yourself from the experience and not take it personally, you may have had a different reaction. You are continually looking for a solution, but constantly meeting with challenges that put you against a double-edged blade. There's no way someone can tell you what to do, because you are the only person who knows exactly what is needed to resolve it. Others cannot help you or they do not know how to advise you. They do not know whether you should be kind, gentle, or whether you need to be calm, lucid in your mind and speak out about the unfairness. For some people, speaking out is a means of opening a channel of communication, others choose stillness as what they prefer. It has to do with your beliefs, habitual reactions and your willingness to soften the whole situation and this causes you to have a change of attitude. It is the clash between the gloomy ego-self and the little angel within who presents us with these problems and challenges.

You can make contact with the angel at any time in your life by practicing a personal inner connection and not trusting and relying upon someone else's advice: you have the power, wisdom and aptitude within and you yourself will determine the best way to open that portal a little wider or whether you prefer to stay in stillness and calmness.

Although we like the little angel within, sometimes we wish it would disappear and leave us alone. However, it won't go away, or stay silent, and somehow the little angel transforms itself to become more active and offer you advice on more difficult issues, especially when you are stuck in a situation and have no exit. The little angel will show you through signs and insight, and it will guide you to see where the trouble and unfavorable surroundings are hidden and navigate you out of the adverse situation so that you can have your troubles resolved in a calm and peaceful manner without further ado.

Therefore, you must be grateful for everything and everyone that helps you to evolve and continue to evolve. In fact, we are inevitably evolving all the time with an ever-lasting, growing and infinite spirit. We will always learn new things as new challengers appear to challenge us almost moment-by-moment: that teaches us to get better and change our attitudes in a situation so that we always stay in consciousness with our eyes to see and ears to hear every stimulus that is around us and get out of complex situations very quickly.

When we feel gratitude to everyone we are like a child again, trusting and loving everything with love, kindness and compassion. Everyone loves everyone: we are full of hope, full of aspirations, full of expectations and goodness. However, the situation has slowly changed since we grew up and has transformed to become less endurable, with less love and care for each other. All the trust and faith that we built up had been lost into the thin air and replaced by greed, envy and jealousy that destroys us as we are consequently misaligned with the Universal Source because we do not recognize our true identity.

You must keep an open mind so that you can perceive each

situation differently and afresh. You must treat every situation equally as if you had never dealt with similar ones previously, with a fully new approach and interpretation. In this way you will not mistreat or ignore anyone: rather you will welcome everyone that enters onto your path and that's how we learn. You open your heart to everyone and confer benefits to all. It is a continuous learning process and a continual journey of vigilance.

One thing, though, we should not do is try to change others without transforming ourselves. We cannot change others so they live an ideal life according to our own interpretation and expectation because it does not work this way. Trying to change others or set goals for others is like interfering with someone else's privacy without permission and can be very aggressive. In fact, its the real meaning is to create more success for ourselves with an ego's version of showing off to others. When we do this to others, we are forcefully trying to change others: we are asking them to live up to our own standards and ideals. Instead, we should merely be kind and love them, and indirectly help and guide them to see joy and happiness through our example and stimulus. Then, we will achieve more successes because, when we help others to succeed, then we will become more successful. That is the real meaning of success: always sends love, kindness and compassion to others through your awareness so everyone can enjoy all that it brings as it adds more vivid colors to people's lives and lets them be filled with their own gifts, energy, inspiration, empowerment, freedom, guidance, aptitude, qualities and clarity and ultimately they move forward by themselves freely, effectively and fearlessly.

Sometimes you want to get rid of situations that drive you crazy, but you cannot, especially when the voice inside attempts to speak to you. However, you realize that sweet things happen when you least expect them. You are grateful to the soft voice within that helps you to solve the problem and not hurt anymore. But, the gloomy voice treats you so badly that you just want to find the way out. You do not want to listen to the gloomy ego's dark voice that makes you feel so bad and abused or degraded and humiliated.

When you realize you have triggered the power within, you want to keep it and do not want to lose it. You know the soft voice is a benefit to you and can guide your energy where you want it to be. You have the aptitude to know how to make conscious connections with the innate power consistently. You have, before you entered the planet Earth, somehow for some unknown reason, got caught up by the gloomy ego and become stuck in the middle: then you surrender to what is in order to communicate rather than be resistant.

We are thinking all the time: as a result, many thoughts come to us without our oversight, without our filtering them or even catching them. If it can, still some unthought-of pessimistic energy will find a loophole that you do not know about and enter the mind: then you are stuck with negative thoughts. In some cases, especially when you are in a negative mood with low energy, it gets through easily, reversing your original thoughts and substituting them with more negative emotions and feelings. Consequently, what you think will create your own reality and transfer itself into negative desires.

You do not know that you are stuck with negative emotional thoughts because you have been compromised by your negative friends in your mind. You only feel what gets through to your mind at the present time: that the negative entities are controlling you and could destroy you. This is guided by the gloomy ego that led you into diving deeper into the negative energy thought field, unaware of being compromised by negative poisonous ingredients. The quiet moment when you get reconnected to the softened hot spot reminds you, however, that you are on a negative path: then you wake up to consciousness and the ego becomes smaller and disappears. Through the silence and stillness your compassion kicks in and you are awakened to the now and are able to reverse the negative thoughts, redirecting them to the higher energy thought field, regaining your consciousness in the present time by positive thinking and staying alert.

Once upon a time, there was a man I met and he told me that he was really kind and compassionate by nature, so I decided he would not be annoying enough to fight back. I tested him with my mean-tempered and negative emotions. I felt that was the only way I could test him so I could stay aware and vigilant of his response. Fortunately, I did not need to test him because in reality he was not as pleasant as he had said.

In our own reality, he is the person who, when you invite him through the front door, will go right down into your home's basement and find out what you have and mark it down or pick up one of these things, bring it up to you and say, "I found you possess a couple these items in your store box: may I have one, if you do not mind?"

This person looks familiar to you: you may have met someone like this in the waking hours of your life. You possibly may think you are in no way like him. The greedy minds of others are the reflection of our own inner self: you simply zoom in and see it all. It is a way to learn and reflect: in them you make transformations in yourselves. So, you call the ego and the angel together for a meeting to discuss the issue regarding a bad habit of yours. You think it is time to deal with the problem so you sit and talk about what a creep your ego-self is and confront the ego. The ego thinks it is right to keep the item since the person does not use it and you should have it, while the angel argues that the ego has no right to take someone else's possession, even though the item is sitting there in the box. To grab someone else's wealth or property is damn wrong. You like to do that because of greed and jealous thoughts craved in the mind and, mostly, you are encouraged and guided by the ego. You have absolutely no right to take away others' property because you want and desire it. Other people's property does not belong to you and you should eliminate those un-thought of thoughts. The two parties continue to argue who's right and who's wrong. The true fact is nobody ever encourages you to allow yourself to feel greed and envy of others' wealth and hurt yourself, but you can try to figure out what is the right path that you should follow.

There is a television program called "Hell's Kitchen." In the "Hell's Kitchen" are twenty students trained to become the ultimate chef in France. All the chefs come there to learn from this infamous chef. One of his main methods of training is to be awake to whatever process you are in. He likes to be very serious and perfect with his students. He could be very mean in his use of language to make you feel bad and hurt. At the end of the program, eighteen of his students will be eliminated and only two remain to compete against each other. The two will have opportunities to design their own kitchen and prepared for a great night in order to succeed. The ultimate prize is that the winner will own that restaurant to become the number one chef in France.

This story tells us that without the negative ego, we do not know how to make transformations in the four pillars of our life. The ego may serve to awaken us to face challenges, despair, panic, adversity, catastrophe and emergencies. However, negative and positive should be in balance in our lives to make life more interesting and rewarding. Therefore, be grateful to all that we learn from each other to improve life on Earth. Give gratitude to every organism here and to the creator that give us life. We should appreciate Him for His might and grace, bless us, one day we may live in harmony with one another without conflict or war, but feel love and compassion for each other through the power within.

Chapter Twelve
Living in Consciousness

It is not true that you can't live in the now. The ego mind prefers to stay in the past and dwells on the fluid future, but denies the present moment. The mind wants to continue to be in control, but in a timeless way, which is the past and future, so it sees that the eternal is frightening. That is when past memories always recur to you when you do not need them. The past cannot be validated as real, but it is only a delusion that has no merit: therefore, you need to start living in the moment that you enjoy, however, you must see it for yourself as nobody can tell you what to do with your life.

Furthermore, you cannot vibrate any energy created in the past and transfer it to the fluid future because it does not exist in the present. The future comes only when the present enters the future, then it becomes your present. For example: if you were abused in your childhood, that happened in the past, but now it still has repercussions in your everyday life even though you know that you are not hurting anymore in consciousness, so you should have no fears or pains except that you aware of the terrible memories are still revisiting you that hurt you within and are real. However, if you stop thinking of the past and refuse to accept it all, feel pity yourself and hug what was experienced as your truth, then you can feel joy and tranquility in the consciousness of your true being. Remember, the more you contemplate, embrace and focus on negative thought emotions, the more you have given the power away to the ego or to others, and more hurtful feelings will emerge to you. You become the hostage controlled by your ego. When you are controlled by the ego, you are in a state of unhappiness and lose your freedom, and everything you perceive becomes negative, and with your influence, thought processes and pessimistic emotions turn a small personal problem into more pain, grief and discontentment. You disconnect from your friends and relatives. You lose your true identity as an infinite being and ultimately you will also lose everything dear to you unless you stay alert, liberated and forgive yourself: shift your past to the deep consciousness and start living in the now. When you dwell in the past, a positive activity you often do will also be stopped because you lose interest: as an alternative you tune into alcohol and drugs in an attempt to remove and ease the sadness, misery and hurtful suppressed feelings within. An old poem says it perfectly, "Using alcohol to resolve and excuse your troubles will bring more grief into your life." Alcohol and drugs cannot lift your current dilemma, rather you become filled with addiction and that only happens in a relatively short period of time and leaves you with no relief. You must awaken in the now and seek relief in the now.

Past memories are only an illusion and anything that is not concrete or built on rock has no foundation, so if you continuously live in the unreal past, it will create more problems for you in the present and everything you do will turn lemon yellow. You create more troubles for yourself, you are continuously hurting yourself and affecting others around you and the world.

When you continuously live in the delusional past, it pleases the ego that you unconsciously maintain your habitual and wrong beliefs and deny that of have created the unease and discontentment: you defied the truth and accepted it as normal living. Because you are not resisting what the ego recommends, it raises no threat to the ego, but gradually it brings up anger, fear, aggregation, and depression and pain for your physical body: this has been triggered, consequently you become habituated to it. You feel that you are not living in reality; you realize that you are out of touch and are conscious that your entire life is observed by the gloomy ego. You are really stuck by the ego-led life. You no longer feel connected to the compassionate and kind heart that dwells within: rather you feel tremendous pain as opposed to bliss, cheerfulness and happiness. What is reality is all included in your healthy well-being so that you experience joy from within and express it to the external world: you possessed happiness, therefore, you can attain everything.

If you cannot stay in the now, even in a normal surroundings such as when you are at your home sitting by yourself alone, walking in the forest, or listening to the radio, then you definitely won't be able to stay alert as to your mind is contemplating something else when something happens or you face difficult situations or people: then you will be compromised by panicking, usually in the form of fear and being dragged into deep unconsciousness. These challenge test your awareness. You deal with them unwaveringly and show others where you are at as far as your condition of consciousness is concerned, but do not sit down there with your eyes closed and envision that the situation will fade.

Therefore, it is important to bring more vivid colors of consciousness into your life in ordinary circumstances where everything is going relatively easily and effortlessly. So, you continuously live in the present and evolve and develop in the dynamic power of the present. It creates an energy field in you of a higher vibrational energy from above and below and around you. You are being protected and shielded from unconsciousness and no negativity can enter the Higher Consciousness Energy Thought Field as the darkness cannot survive in the omnipresence of Divine Light Power.

When you continuously observe and monitor your vibrational emotional thoughts in the present you will be surprised for the very first time how rarely you are always truly at ease within yourself. You hear of a lot of background noises and the resistant force in the form of judgment, discontentment and the mind's projection that is distant from the now. Emotionally you will feel unease, tension and anxiety. However, these negative aspects are the projection of the mind in its customary resistant form.

Why are we as anxious as we go along in our daily living? It is because we can't stop carving and creating thoughts in the mind in order to create the things we want unceasingly. We always seek and desire things in our mind through the power of thought vibrations. We have never stopped wanting and craving: that causes us to be anxious, nervousness and uneasy, and it will continue to be so because it is our nature to crave thoughts and inevitably we want and seek something: it has a long history and existed in both Eastern and Western culture and is manifested in an unprecedentedly heightened form.

Being resistant to living in the Now will cause a loss of

connection with your real self as an Infinite Being. As Infinite creative being, you are always living in awareness and you have unlimited power always to create things in creative consciousness. You recognize the root of your true nature and realize the freedom of creating everything and transforming it so it becomes possible and available to you in the present time. This brings joy and happiness as opposed to fear and fright. This awareness has become a harmonized and peaceful ally not only in itself but also to every organism and life on planet Earth.

When you are living in the present moment, your creative power is in the Now and not in the future or the past. The timeless present has limitless creative potential while nothing can be created again in the illusion of the past and nothing will happen in the unfolding future, but it will happen in the eternal present. Consciousness is the key to your spiritual evolution and development and ever-lasting and eternal life.

The choice is yours to make: you should live in the Now because when you think of the past it is only a memory recorded in the subconscious. When you retrieve data recorded in the subconscious, you actually recall memories from the past, but you do so in consciousness, in the here and now. While the future is still creating an imagination stimulus, it is a projection of the mind. When the future comes, it comes in the consciousness, in the potential Now. You think and decide what to do tomorrow in the present moment, not in the illusionary past. Visibly the past and the future possess no real merit because they have no sense of being real and validated. Therefore, the past and future in reality is utilized for the glory of the light in the timeless present. Although the mind can never appreciate the eternal present, time and mind can never be separated. Time and mind rely upon each other to survive in the creative consciousness and radiate energy to the Infinite Being from the mind, and from time to the Now, and make everything feel dynamic and infinite.

People like mountain climbing, car racing, and other dangerous activities because of the excitement of that moment: then they are free from thinking and just keep going until they reach the mountain-top or the race ends. There is danger involved, but it forces them to awaken to the awareness of the Now. But, you do not need to do that: you can always enter that state of the present and enjoy the pleasure of deliberate consciousness in the present.

The present moment has no time, no scarcity, no pain and no suffering. It only wants to awaken you and to direct and catch your attention totally in the Now. You must be aware that scarcity, pain and suffering need time to be fulfilled and time to heal, but feeling a lack, pain or suffering is not the real you: when you connect to your real being, you have no suffering, no pain and no lack. All problems are resolved in the absence of time and in consciousness of God's presence. God is timeless; God has no beginning and no end. Therefore, God is the infinite present and we align with Him in the Now to obtain a profound inner peace and tranquility. Be vigilant: the past and future cover our vision of God; cancel them in consciousness.

Now, silence the mind for a moment. Then you ask yourself some questions, "What's going on inside me at the present time? Am I at the moment content with my Inner Being so I know what I feel and project it to the outside?" When I am calm and peaceful within then everything outside will follow. Halt for a moment. Inhale and exhale deeply. Then you feel the reality within. Next, you feel the reality externally. You do not need to rush in to answer these questions. Slowly draw your attention inward. Dive within yourself. What kind of thought is your mind craving? What do you feel? Do you feel tension inside? Do you feel any resistance or unease in your mind? Do you try to avoid or deny something in your life? Perhaps you refuse to live in consciousness, in the here and now. Do you still hold resentment against the person you are averse to, even if he is long gone? When you practice in silence and observe your inner consciousness, you will get awareness and answers to the above questions.

Do you know what is real? Reality is when you feel joy you attain a profound well-being both inside and outside. Both the internal and external mixed together becomes one joyful and happy being. You truly feel the joy and blissfulness within and are constantly connected with the kind heart which transcends the goals of attainment and fulfillment, as you are whole with the Universal Source. You truly know yourself as an Infinite Being and you do not need desire to create happiness since you already have everything in the conscious Now. You have taken your mind and returned to the Universal Source to point zero: that is purity, void and emptiness. You blend with the Source as you continue your journey on Earth.

Do you resent doing what you are doing? Perhaps you resent your current job or maybe a job you promised to do, but deep within you resist and resent it. Are you holding resentment against a person you are averse to even after he had long gone? Do you understand that you contaminate your energy and are hurting yourself as well as those around you? Now look from within. Is there resentment hiding inside? If there is, you observe it both at the internal and external emotional levels. What thoughts are created in the mind that causes you to hold the resentment for this long? Then, feel the body's reaction to those emotional thoughts. Does it still feel pain and unpleasantness? Is it an energy you choose to keep inside you? Do you have a choice? Maybe it is time to let go of the negative emotions:

whether they are justified or not make no difference. You are creating the present moment as so unpleasant. You are continuously creating unhappiness for yourself and your own Inner Being and those around you and the world. You have polluted the world without taking responsibility for your inner world. You must drop this resentment and forgive yourself: enter into the unwanted situation that is hurting you and move on. Do not let this resentment hold you back with bad energy as you are stuck in the past filled with pain and unhappiness. Unhappiness can spread faster than a disease. Through collective consciousness it triggers and transcends through the air into the atmosphere and affects other souls, unless they have shields against negativity and so are protected.

You must drop your selfish mind and turn off the resentment and eliminate the suppression within and clean yourself in consciousness. When you clean the suppression within, at the same time you create a clean environment without. So, you do it for your own good and the world appreciates you.

By recognizing and awakening in consciousness that you do not want to suffer the pain and sustain the burden any longer, you then surrender to the Source. This awareness can happen all of a sudden and awaken you from deep unconsciousness, as you do not need to carry on that deep pain and can transmute it through alignment with the Source and your inner presence. Your constant attention in consciousness can alert you to stay out of trouble and see clearly what is around you. Usually you drop one that hurts you most: eventually you recognize you do not need them anymore and understand you have a choice to live in the present or continue to live in the painful past. You can do this because you are awakened in the Now. Without the present you do not have a choice. The past is lifeless. You do not need it. Only refer to it when it is relevant to the present. Now, feel the fullness of the Infinite Being, feel your presence and the power of the present moment fearlessly.

Sometimes we spend most of our life waiting for prosperity to come, but most of the time we are disappointed because we are expecting something happen in the future. There is nothing wrong in hoping for a change. You can change your life's conditions but you cannot change your life because your life was already perfect and whole when God created you. You should be fully living in the present reality and appreciate what you have already received and are grateful in the present moment and live life to the full in the Now: that is true prosperity. Prosperity comes to you in many different ways when you least expect it and when the time is mature.

If you are not happy with what you have already and continue feeling a lack, then you will continue to attract more dissatisfactions to you. Even though you may lucky enough when winning a lottery and you become a millionaire, deep down you will continue feel unfulfilled. You may be excited about all that money can buy, but money comes and goes and always leaves you with an empty feeling and the need for more gratification and mental support. You want to stand for your own Being and so begin to live life in the fullness that alone is true prosperity.

Our journey on Earth has two purposes to fulfill: an inner purpose and outer purpose. The inner purpose concerns the deepening of your Inner Source by a directly vertical connection with the Universal Source in consciousness in the here and now. The inner purpose is always guiding you in the present moment. It walks with you through the external recognition of your ultimate destination. You set goals and desires that you want in your life and you accomplish them through the power within. The mind projects your desires to the external world through the horizontal dimension and transforms your dream into profoundly reality when the time is right. Obviously, you realize that most of our goals and desires are set to be accomplished in the future, rather achieved in the Now. So, if we want to create new projects then we must create them in the current moment: you do not need to wait for the future to do it. When the future comes, it would be too late. You should direct your attention with the quality of consciousness in the moment. Any moment is the right moment to create the desire you set out, then everything will fall into place. Then, you won't miss the inner journey which always occurs in the present moment. Your inner purpose is always focusing on and fulfills everything in the timeless Now. It is the journey that we are taking right at this moment. As soon as you realize that your life's purpose is guided by the power within, then your external journey already contains all the power needed that leads you to reach your destination. The combination of both steps will transform the beauty of expression of your Inner Being and shine through everything you want to fulfill. It is the journey fulfilled both internally and externally that is navigated by your own inner power with one purpose in mind: to accomplish the mission and achieve a special purpose and experience the ultimate goal of your own amazing and wonderful journey on Earth.

Remember your life's purpose must be guided by the Inner Source of your own self but not navigated by the external world. The external purpose cannot be fulfilled without the riches of insight from within: even though you may continue enjoy it, pretty quickly you realize that you will fail without internal support. It is according to the Universal Laws of Nature that nothing created in the external can last forever and it is different from the Infinite realm. The external world has the limitations of life spans on Earth and is subject to the Law of Impermanence of all things. Therefore, it is wise to connect with your Inner Being to achieve your joy and happiness and make it humble and inevitably show gratitude to your inner guide.

Now, you know that you should pay more attention to the present and ignore and defy the past and the fluid future which has no true reality and is only an illusion. You should pay more attention to your behavior, to your current reactions to thing around you, your moods, thoughts, speech, emotions, fears and desires, since they occur in the Now. You should stop driving yourself into the past or think of the past or surrender to the past. You perceive yourself coming into the present and living in the moment and the moment is always full of bliss and joyfulness. That is the power of living in consciousness, given you and nothingness, and you will never miss anything and always have the transformative power of peace within.

Maybe you are sitting comfortably and quietly contemplating what your next thought is going to be? So you just sit and wait for the new thought to emerge, but you did not realize that you cannot anticipate the Now. The mind cannot understand the timeless present, but only connect in the past and future. The present is you doing something in consciousness right at this conscious moment without being alert in your mind. For example, you want a cup of tea and you want it now, without thinking too much about it. You do not give time to your mind to interpret it, but you want to drink it in the moment. Often, if you expect something, then it will never arrive. Because you will receive it in the future tense, you hope it will happen but no action has been taken in the conscious Now. You cannot expect something will occur or not in the future. Nothing will occur again in the past and in the fluid future until it unfolds in the here. You can only gain something and motivate it in the Now: then you will receive what you expect to receive. It is true that we spend most of our life waiting for things to arrive, we are on hold, in a traffic jam etc., which is beyond our control: it becomes a part of our daily living, but we do have choices. You are the decider. When you catch yourself waiting, come out of it and guide yourself into the present moment. Just be and enjoy yourself and stay conscious. Still, there are things happening which are within our awareness that is a start for living in the moment, being present. Your conscious presence is important. You do not need to understand the past but be in the moment, stay alert, be as still as you can: that will dissolve the past. The past cannot survive as long as you awaken in your presence. It can only be alive while you are unconscious.

Chapter Thirteen
The Inner Source

The physical body can become an access point into the realm of the Inner Source. Each individual has their own Inner Source, or you may call it the soul or subconscious mind. It is simply a label we put on it in the physical world, but don't get stuck on a word. If you have strong aversion to the words "Inner Source", replace it with the one that speaks to you. Do not be attached to anything, but detached. You may call it whatever you want, and it is your reality and your own awareness. Language is a strange thing: as long as the word is clear enough and close to the truth, and the word "points it out" to you in reality, then use it.

The Inner Source is your deepest conscious self or your own soul living in your physical body and can be felt as always-present, always-evolving, and always-eternal. The body is a temple for your Inner Source and guides, evolves and walks on a mission with you here. It is important that you abide by your own Inner Source to make the journey on Earth become a great success.

The Inner Source is an emotional being, especially when it feels sick inside: that also affects you, so you feel restless outside in the physical world. So, it is important for you to take care of your own soul, as you care for your physical body.

Now, you know that you have something more valuable than your physical body and mind. The illusion of this true identity confuses you because you do not know who-you-really-are, and not knowing your real identity is a huge blunder. Confusion causes conflict in your mind since you already live in a physical world of illusion in which all temporary. The consequence of this confusion is the illusion of fear, as you do not know your true self an Infinite Being. The sooner you realize your true Infinite Self, the sooner you are no longer trapped in the shell and you can envision it more clearly, hear the sound beyond, feel insightful, think and know extraordinary things before they happen and can achieve astral travel to the fourth dimension, which is beyond the comprehension of your conscious mind.

The physical body cannot take you into your Inner Source. The physical body is just the outer shell, which has limitations, and only perception and power in reality. As long as your conscious mind is under your command, you cannot feel your Inner Source. A very effective way to connect with your Inner Source is to removed the attention of the conscious mind and meditate the energy directly into the consciousness of your own soul within. So, you feel the "Inner Source", the life inside the physical body, and thus come to realize that you are beyond the physical form.

Now close your eyes and silence the mind and direct your attention and feel the energy from within. Is there life inside? Do you feel the energy from your hands, arms, shoulders, neck, your throat, cells, blood vessels, your chest, your abdomen, legs and feet? Continue to focus on the subtle energy that is now flowing and vibrating through your whole body, then bring your attention to focus on your Inner Self for a few minutes. But do not think about it as yet! Simply feel it is present. The more attention you give it, the stronger this feeling becomes. It is a feeling as if every cell and vessel is coming alive, and if you have a strong sense of creative visualization, you may experience images emerging to you and feel your body turn glowing. You feel that your entire body is shielded by the white light. Your attention should be set on your feeling in connection with the Inner Source. You want to activate the innate power so you can communicate with it consciously. You can always go back and practice, and go into it more deeply. If you cannot get any feeling on your first attempt, then try again until you can feel it. Say to your Inner Source that you know it is there inside you and you would like to make contact. Halt for a moment. Wait. You may hear a response from the Inner Source. If you do not hear anything from within, do not feel upset, but look for signs and symbols and your intuition that shows you have made contact and the Inner Source has responded to your request.

Perhaps a slight tingling in your hands or shoulders will show an initial contact. Continue to focus on the inner feeling. Your Inner Self is coming alive. You can always practice some more. Now, bring yourself back to awaken from the trance state. Please open your eyes, but keep the feeling to your Inner Self. It is your identity, your true nature, and you will never lose touch with it.

Now let me bring your attention to your physical body, that hosts your Inner Source, the real recognition of your infinite nature. Due to the physical structure of our bodies, they are subject to disease, sickness, pains, grief, sorrow, suffering, old age and death (but death is not the end, it is only an illusion in the physical world). Death only happens to your body but not to the

Inner Self. The Inner Source has no end and no beginning, but is infinite in nature. Your Inner Source is beyond birth and death. Due to the limitations of the conscious mind, we think death is the end of all things and events and it is a misperception of separation from the Source, the creator, the Mind of God. It is not true. Death is an illusionary creation of your ego mind to cover your immoral reality. All reality of your own truth can be found from within: do not be fooled by the Ego that confuses you by saying that death is your final destination. All power and life begin from within and the projection by the mind translates it to the physical world and conveys it to become your own reality.

Do not discriminate against your physical body, for, in doing so, you fight against your own reality. You need the body to host the Inner Source and you must treat your body with respect as well as your soul. Through the body you make contact with the power from within. Your body is like a cover with a veil and underneath there is a powerful source, an invisible self, that connects you to the source of the spiritual realm: the invisible force, the Universal Source of consciousness has no past, it is only consciously present, it has no beginning and no end, it is birthless, deathless and always-present. Through the Inner Source, you infinitely resonate with God. (Moses asked God, "Who are you?" God answered, "I am who I am. I am the alpha and omega, I am omnipresent. I am your Almighty Powerful God.")

Let me bring your attention back to the state of consciousness from within, through permanent connectedness with your Inner Source, so you can feel it inevitably. This will quickly deepen and change your life. The more consciousness you direct into your Inner Source, the higher the frequency of vibration that can be felt from within and can transform to become more active and dynamic: you begin to feel it increases the flow of energy exchanged through your body, then you know it is triggered.

When you connect with the higher energy flow, no negativity can enter your mind that can affect you because the mind is taken over by the Inner Source and you are actually out of the third dimension and have moved into the fourth dimension, into the Universal Source, the Mind of God. You may want to maintain this higher frequency contact frequently so that you are always consciously aligned with the Source, the Mind of God, in order to attain your desires and needs in the physical world and feel the endurance of the transformative power of peace from within. You won't confuse yourself with the external world anymore and you won't lose control to your conscious mind. Thought, emotions, fear, and desire are constantly there, but you know now you can resolve these problems by extending the power within and allowing the Innate Power take you over. The power is within you forever and this is the power God has given you.

Now examine where your attention is at this present moment. You are reading these words in my book. It means you are focusing your attention. You are aware of your environment, the people around you, and other activities (you may hear noises from outside etc.). Yet you should defy the other noises that are not worth catching your attention. Try to pay attention to both the internal and external attention at the same time. Continue to keep your attention on the inner self. Withhold some of your inner energy. Do not let it all flow out. Feel the whole body from inside as one source of energy. It is almost as though you were listening and reading with your entire body from within. You can continue practicing making contact with your Inner Source until the contact is activated and triggered.

When practicing consciously connection to the power from within, it is important that you do not give away all your attention to your mind and the outside world. You may continue to focus on your daily activities, but feel the Inner Source at the same time whenever possible. Remember to stay original within. Then, be vigilant about how this transforms your state of consciousness and the quality of your daily activities. Take whatever time possible to feel the Inner Self. Feel that the Inner Self is present in the Now by going more deeply inside into the body.

The more you practice observing from the inside and bringing your awareness to the present, the more you will develop a new way of living, of being permanently connected with the Inner Self. This will add more vivid colors to your daily living such as you have never experienced before. Most of the time you feel calm and serene and continue to run your mind from the inside and let the mind project what you release from the inside to the external world in consciousness, but you inevitably stay rooted within and you begin to create a solid foundation: everything is according to your heart's desire. It is like a tree that is deeply grounded in the earth or a building with solid foundations dug deep and founded on rock: then you build a house which can withstand the flood and wind.

If at any moment you find it difficult to connect with the Inner Source, try to practice breathing exercises first as it will help you get in touch with your physical body through the practice of meditation. Pay attention to inhaling and exhaling out of your body. If you can sense the visual, then close your eyes and perceive yourself surrounded by a white light that covers your whole body—a deep consciousness. Take breaths in the light. Feel the light fill up your whole body and make it shine. Then, slowly focus more on the conscious feeling. You are now in your body. Then, continue to focus more on your emotions, but be detached from any creative image.

If you want to use your mind for a specific purpose, blend it with your Inner Source. When you are conscious with thoughtlessness then you can use your mind because your mind is empty. You can use your mind appropriately and creatively and it is an easier step to enter the state of emptiness through your body. Halt for a moment and stop thinking for a moment, but focus your attention on your inner vibration. Become aware of the motionlessness. When you resume thinking, it will be fresh and creative. When you are ready to crave thoughts, make it habitual to think and then stop and go back to the thought again, back and forth, and pay special attention to the thought and a kind of listening within, and an inner silence. It is as when you crave your thoughts: you think with your whole body and invite the Inner Self to assist you but it is not just thinking alone.

When the mind is running your life, conflict, fear, and problems are unavoidable. However, constantly keeping in touch with your Inner Light and entering into the sacred gap of thoughtlessness within means that the relationship can blossom.

Chapter Fourteen
Conquering an Obstacle

Before we arrived here, we signed an accord with the Source to take on every task whether pleasant or unpleasant, and every challenge, excitement, contentment, element of joy or peace and to complete them after we arrive on planet Earth. However, you possess free will not to abide by this and blow it, to walk on a total opposite life path, to make friends with the darkness. Then eventually you come to your senses and you want an exit and to walk on the right direction, so you can complete your whole mission on Earth.

Although you possess the power to decide what you want to create, the Universe is standing by ready to bless you and allow things to happen when you invite the Source to help. This happens especially when you stand at a crossroads and do not know what to do, feeling uncertainty in a circumstance or that your life is in danger or that you are lost in a desert with no way of knowing your direction. When all this happens, you request the invisible to open up a path, you surrender to what you hold you back to the unknown Universe and let go of attachments.

You become completely detached so the Source can remove you to safety so that you will be free from harm. The Source cannot lend a hand if you want to be in control at the same time and you must submit and wait patiently because everything follows a sequence that cannot be hurried: until it occurs, you must believe a transformation has begun, but you can inevitably raise your awareness to harness the present. Now, you must relax so you can find signs and receive inspiration, turn them into action, reverse your adverse situations and dissolve them in an unwavering manner and transmute your wildest dreams into the concrete reality you deserve.

There are driving forces in the unknown Universe that can cause obstacles to occur to us partly because of our unawareness and also due to pessimistic thoughts and emotions, or bad or wrong actions taken by us without thinking them through properly and appropriately. We allow our mind to think freely without blending it and consulting with the Inner Source and the mind guides us by walking in the wrong direction until we realize it is too late to reverse that.

It is the habitual behavior that you use on a daily basis to control your business, your finances and other regular activities that you do in normal circumstances that are problematic: you do not see anything wrong until something unpreventable occurs to you. Then you realize mistakes have been made that hold you back from success and take away your joy, happiness and affect your good health or another area of your life.

Experience tells us that when something goes wrong, we try to change it, but we failed because we followed a previous pattern or older belief that is already been out of date and yet we thought we could still implement it to give a quick fix: this relies upon the force of the outside world.

So, we tried but failed. Then, we tried again until we dropped. Sooner or later, we abandoned all resistance, and then everything began to turn around and open a new portal to us. The things that we love, or did previously become disinteresting to us and even repulsive, then suddenly we realized that we do not need to fight against it anymore: non-resistance makes it possible for you to dissolve problems easily, quickly and without effort.

Negative emotions and depression are the greatest enemies we face daily, but how can we thrust them out of our lives so everything be easier for us without experiencing more pains and sadness? In fact, we do not need to cast them out, but rather choose to make friends with them: the sooner you befriend your negative emotions, the sooner you can direct and reverse them to positive emotions. With positive emotions, you speak and act more confidently and your life is no longer out of touch and beyond control and comprehension.

Your emotions control every single aspect of your behavior: how you think, talk, and act, connect, your personality, your character, your temperament, your likes or dislikes, and the way you dress, the color you like, the music you listen to, your diet and the people you resonate with and ultimately how you react when you face a difficult situation and circumstance.

The reason we are stuck in an event or circumstance is because the conscious mind likes to stay in the past and is afraid of consciousness in the present. The mind does not like the infinite present because it is a timeless present and so it chooses to stay in the illusionary past to feel safe, and so it can send you more problems or guide you to move to the unfolding future as nothing ever happens, and so it can always track the time and control you. However, we cannot remove time from the mind, it ceases to operate, yet we still need to use it. Time and mind are inseparable.

We stick by our emotions because we don't direct our minds to positive thoughts: immediately we feel negative emotions emerge for us. We allow it to stay with us continuously and believe that it is beyond our powers to change it and so accept it as is. Eventually, it becomes a habit and we accept it as true; then we can't change it anymore. It is untrue because emotions are dynamic and ongoing and change all the time. We are emotional beings, easily affected by the external environment, in our moods within and attitude to perceiving things. When we perceive something that we like, then we are happy and feel joy from within but when something upsets us immediately we become very emotional and turn to negative thoughts and actions. Since emotion is an ongoing process and we can change it at any time we want and substitute it with joy and happiness. For example, if you do not like a particular place, you stop going there, if you do not like a particular store, you stop shopping there. If people do not resonate with you and cause you upset, disconnect with them forever. If you do not like a particular kind of thinking pattern or habit, change it with your Inner Source so you crave better thoughts and get your desires in consciousness in the present.

We must be vigilant about the language that we choose in our inner dialogue as that may have a profound influence on our daily living. For example, I do not want to get up, I feel tired with no energy. I do not want to go to work. Perhaps I call in sick. Compare it to, "Huh! I feel energetic this morning! I must get out of bed and be ready to go to work. I enjoy every bit of work I do and am eagerly looking forward to returning to work as soon as I am ready!" Another negative emotion that you agreed to, "Well, I do not think I am getting better…my illness is getting worse as time goes by." The language that we use with ourselves must be selected because it can serve as self-hypnosis that can run our lives.

When you feel negative emotion, it may not be a bad thing because it urges you to make transformational changes and pay attention to your body. You are feeling sick, tired, stressed, and depressed—these are the signs that your body tells you to stop and get more rest so your body can rejuvenate and feel alive again. The sooner you make these changes, the sooner your body feels that it is loved, feels harmony and peace, cheerful and grateful. You have just turned on the power inside to make yourself feel dynamic and exchanged energetic emotions triggered from within.

Some people believe they cannot change their lives because of chemical imbalances: that is untrue. You can change your emotions which are under your control from within and, with the help of the Inner Source, you can use your negative emotions to improve your life, especially when you recognize that part of your life is no longer valid and was in the past. The past is gone and not dynamic: it can never hurt you again. Now, try to revisit that painful past and perceive that you are not afraid of facing and confronting that event and those people and so you are able to break the bond and close that Chapter of your book.

If you can see visions, you can imagine you have spun that negative emotion out of your body from the crown to root chakra. Notice it spins forward and backward, negative and positive, up and down three times, then you push it out of your body forever. Then, come back to the present with a fresh, positive and joyful emotion: realize that you now have a positive sense that enriches life and you have more reason to live than you thought of : anything you no longer need you can surrender to nature and detach from. You are a new you and believe you can have joy and happiness in your life like everybody does. Do not go back, and never regret what happened and carry on your life. If negative emotions recur to you again, give them a smile and say, "Hah huh! You can't hurt me anymore because you are gone and dropped." Your past were healed and you can move beyond it without fear. You accept and love yourself unconditionally and unwaveringly: you have changed your thinking patterns and beliefs to confirm that you changed. You live in consciousness in the here and now. You are alive! You move forward to live your dream fearlessly and abundantly.

Any unwanted struggle and circumstance has the power to stay alive for a very long time. In order to eliminate struggle or fighting or resistance, it is important to create and accumulate merit. The way to accumulate value is to be willing to give something to help others, be willing to give generously, be willing not to hold back. It is explained as letting go: by holding on to yourself, you are letting go of your self-centered ego. In fact, when you are willing to detach from everything you love or enjoy instead of keeping it to yourself, you give it all away and begin to experience your world and more new friends approach you. That is true value.

What is true value? A true value is to open, to give and not hold back and shield yourself from anything; instead you open your heart and let the entire thing dissolve. That is how value is built up.

You can do all sorts of thing to accumulate your merit, such as donating money or offering volunteer services to others. If you offer things to these worthy causes, with real generosity and you give without asking for anything particular in return, that is to abide by the Universal Laws of Giving and Receiving. The real giving is that you are giving something you love: you may find it difficult to give it away in the beginning, but as you start to give and feel the inner joy and bliss, then you know it is the right thing to do. There should be no resentment and no fearfulness, but the pure intention of giving to help others. Then again, it may reduce your karmic debts if you have accumulated those over the years. Nevertheless, a good deed has been recorded in the Book of Karma in your name. If the Universe grants you blessings, then you must deserve to receive it, let yourself be blessed. It is not that you give money away with an intention to receive blessings, but you simply ask the Universe to grant the blessings and hope it happens, and let it happen.

Surrender, let go of acquisitions and detach: these are all synonyms for building up merit. The idea is to open your wealth and share it with the needy, rather than close the door and be unwilling to donate: let the flow of life energy continue through dynamic exchange.

Confess to your blunders as this will help remove your inner struggle, any suppression and resistance. You regret what you have done to yourself and promise not to commit it again. Chant mantras thousands of times, meditate on God and seek forgiveness from yourself. Express complete willingness in the present not to commit such foolish actions again and continue to practice good deeds to lessen your faults, regret, and resolve not to repeat them again.

Bad circumstances happen all the time and it may not be your fault that you have unconsciously connected yourself with the unthought-of circumstance and got hurt, but you know that you can transform them. You do not need to confess to anybody; it's nobody business but a personal matter. You have not committed any criminal act. You look at yourself, what you did and go through the process and clean it within. You do not need anyone to forgive you. You forgive yourself by saying to yourself, "I am sorry I hurt you, please forgive me and I love you. Thank you." After that you do not have that fear anymore and you do not need to lock yourself into a room and put bolts on the door. You simply remove your thin veil and stop covering yourself with dark glasses and body armor.

Confessing your fearful action is to do an honest action that will help your build a new life by eradicating the thin veil, the dark glasses, and taking off that protective shield so you experience the truth fully. You let go of the past and let go of withholding and denying and you open yourself to the world rather than hiding yourself in a closet.

When you regret, you begin to see and become aware of what you do, so you no longer need to hide from yourself. That leads you to see clearly that being fearful is unnecessary, but most importantly, not to blame yourself rather do something that benefits you. Regret implies that you will not do it again and you tire of wearing the transitional glasses, and hiding behind the thin veil and wearing that shield and craving poisonous thoughts against others, you tire of criticizing someone you are adverse to, you are sick of complaining to yourself. Nobody is telling you what to do or is giving you an evil eye. It is you yourself who is getting tired of your illusion of fear and your fearful personality need to be changed. That is, you yearn to make changes to yourself, you acknowledge what you do is at fault and truly regret what you did, rather than continuing to harm somebody and deny it.

You regret your previous action, but now you refrain from doing it again. You know that past actions hurt you so much and you restrain yourself from doing them again. You are not unkind to yourself, you are non-violent, but make a wise decision from within. It's very gentle and decisive, and you say to yourself: "I intend not pushing it, I intent to change and improve one day at a time."

You have done regret. Now you take fearless action to complete the whole confessing process. Taking fearless action is as though you water your plant so it continues to grow and evolve: let go of the past that holds you back as you have a sense of regret, refrain and practice so you purify the whole situation through chanting mantras and through meditation on God. You take refuge in God and surrender what hold you back. You take refuge in a community for support, you do it yourself and this is how you make transformational changes to speed up the process of improving yourself and you no longer need to regret. You have totally forgiven yourself and see yourself grow and keep going. Your resolution is to forgive yourself and remind yourself not to repeat those actions. That is your vow and you do it with confidence, with a sense of appreciation and respect for yourself, and this opens you to nature and provides complete surrender to the powerful Universal Source, the Mind of God.

Chapter Fifteen
Meditation

Yes, you can meditate! Anything you can do, I can do without hesitation and do it better. Who says you cannot? All you need to do is do it without wavering and you will see results. It is a long-term practice, but can have short-term goals and desires.

Meditation can help you to improve your personality, attitude, health, relationships, and enhance and uplift the four pillars of your whole life to the outer limits of the connection and you can experience being both vertical to the Source and tied horizontally to the external world, so you no longer feel confused and inevitably stay in the present moment.

Meditation opens you to learn to be patient, endure, appreciate and realize everything has a time sequence and cannot be pushed fast forward, but you can always awaken things through awareness and interruption: be yourself and enjoy the conscious moment while you are waiting for things to come to you.

Through incentives and the practice of meditation you have

activated the power within, become attuned to your soul, perceived clearly regarding your purposes and about events, understood your soul and align with your soul and made connections to the soul of others and known that you are not alone: you have a soul inside to accompany you on your journey and you are learning lessons on Earth.

When you consider that your practice is a success, you can achieve something after a session of meditation. The primary purpose of meditation is to achieve the quality of acknowledgment in the present moment and ensure that our minds inevitably stay in the here and now. We cannot let our minds wonder back to the past or fast forward into the fluid future which does not yet exist. You should not give any time limits to your practice and should always remain in consciousness in the present moment: when you finish your practice you should stay continuously in awareness in the Now. You go back to your daily life, but stay aware of being in the present and keep your mind in the moment so that you are always awakened in consciousness so it fills you in the present and creates a strong concentration of the awareness of your environment and a clear understanding of the mind regarding reality. You can take control with your mind in practice by sending your mind out to the present moment and calling it back constantly until you have total control your mind from one moment to the next. We can also fix our minds and to stop them doing things freely without being allowed or our desire. Stop the mind doing things which it chooses to do. You guide your mind always to stay in consciousness in the present.

To facilitate the control of our minds, we focus on consciousness, but there are five practices that have to balance with each other. These five practices are beneficial to us when we implement them in our daily living. The five practices are self-confidence, effort/intention, mindfulness, concentration and wisdom. For example, some people may have strong confidence when they give speeches to a public audience, but privately they may possess weakness in the area of creating loving relationships and may need to improve them and continuously work on them. The problem is deep within: they are afraid of being rejected. Rejection is a heartfelt word and hurts our emotions and confidence and prevents us from achieving things we desire. There are reasons for others to reject you. But, it is not your fault because the person did not know you well and you have not met her before: rather you presented yourself in that moment very poorly with a lack of faith in yourself, combined with her prejudgment, prejudice, likes or dislikes in the first three minutes after meeting you. Other reasons are that your soul is aware you do not resonate with her consciousness, therefore you fail to attract the person you want to be with. Hence, it is very important that we can connect with people who consciously resonate with our souls: that would make our lives easy, comfortable, and confident and we will be able to endure things better than we thought: with full confidence you will arise on the horizon and out of the ashes, flying into the sky like a phoenix.

To reach and attract something into our lives, we must acknowledge the true intention of our desire, and have faith and do transforming actions to bring it ultimately into reality in the outside world: we convert desires via the conscious mind and they are reflected as money, success, health, love and wealth. Without intention and effort, you cannot achieve anything, but with them, you never give up your attitude and mix with the inner aptitude to visualize an image: you put forward something fulfilling your desires with intention.

You cannot fail: at least you give effort to doing it and at the end of a session you must achieve a lucid mind in an aware moment. When you are mindful, you are aware of the environment around you. Even when you are not in the room you are still aware of the activities both inside and outside the room: you can hear sounds and use remote viewing to see the room clearly with a lucid mind. You can hear a pin drop on the floor and everything is controlled by you. It is as though you are walking along and, before anything can hit you on the side of the head, you are mindful and alert to the environment so you avoid an accident. The mindfulness of your mind can benefit from a major surprise. With mindfulness, it helps us go through every event, situation and condition in our daily activities. This is especially so with the unexpected events and circumstances that can happen at any conscious moment. It helps you get in touch with your feelings by training your mind: practice inhaling and exhaling exercises that bring your mind to the conscious present. To practice breathing exercises is very helpful to bring out your awareness, especially when you feel stress, anger, resentment or any unwanted negative emotions: breathe in, embrace the present moment, simply be and enjoy yourself and you will remember to breathe out and share a sense of delight and be aware that you just want to be happy.

Some people have an exceptional aptitude to concentration that enables them oversight of everything and brings success into the four areas of their lives. To be able to concentrate is to attain power in the mind that allows you to do anything and accomplish something rapidly without holding back. At the same time, you are able take command of your mind to guide it moment by moment by focusing on consciousness, so the mind will not fall back into the past or wander into the upcoming future. A person, who cannot concentrate due to lack of faith, and confidence and disbelief in himself, has power. That power can bring him almost everything, but only if he applies power from within to concentrate on the work he does and use his mind creatively and wisely. He should use his mind for a special purpose, but it must be in combination with the Inner Consciousness. You use your mind for recalled data, other than that you should use your Inner Self for craving thoughts and every major activity and decision making. Do not let your mind run your life, but control it with the power of inner concentration and focus on the moment. At any given moment you should bring your mind to the present and contemplate in the present, in the here and now.

Your aptitude enables you to accomplish goals, but this depends very much on your inner wisdom, confidence, and faith in yourself to achieve your heart's desire. When you depend on normal wisdom to accomplish your goals and desires, you realize it is very difficult because of your shortcomings due to physical limitations. Your conscious mind has limitations, but the Inner Self has unlimited infinite power, wisdom, and knowledge that can assist you to accomplish anything if you invite it to help you. The Inner Self always attains knowledge, wisdom and energy from the Universal Source, the Mind of God: therefore, its supply of resources is unlimited and never exhausted. Therefore, when you use your mind, blend with the Inner Source: you have increased your learning ability and always remain vigilant and know the importance of bringing the five practices to balance in maintaining concentration. Have confidence, knowing your intention and be mindful of your immediate environment and obtain unlimited wisdom and the ability to succeed.

When you rest your mind, when sitting on a cushion, practice meditation so you can attain wonderful things to you help you to balance the five authorities of confidence, effort, mindfulness, concentration, and wisdom. When you awaken to your normal activities, you can always bring these five authorities with you and utilize them in every area of your life in consciousness in the here and now. Your mind also finds it relaxing and resting in the present moment: that makes you feel the silence and calmness in you and your body feels fresh and connected to nature. Now, you can take on more tasks, create a new project and complete it effortlessly, steadfastly and fearlessly. That is the power of meditation.

Meditation helps you to achieve the experience you want through awareness or mindfulness. Although it cannot be obtained overnight, it is a process gained piece-by-piece over a period of years of practice. It directs certain aspects of your own flowing life experience. Meditation trains you to become more and more receptive to your experiences. You become more sensitive to touch; you see through the opening of your third eye, smell acutely, you can hear your own inner voice and listen to your own thoughts without being caught up in them. Through the process of mindfulness, we gradually become aware of who-we-really are underneath the ego's consciousness. We wake up to what life really is. It is more than just ups and downs or candy on a stick. The physical world is only an illusion. If we do bother to look deep inside the texture, then we look in the right way. Then we discover there is golden treasure living within us which can open up unlimited resources, knowledge, and wisdom beyond the comprehension of our conscious mind.

Through a long-term meditation exercise, you begin to realize what is genuinely happening around and within you. In order to succeed in meditation, your practice must be approached with this attitude. You should not care less for what you have been taught. Eliminate theories and stereotypes. You just want to understand the true meaning of life. You want to experience the meaning of what being alive really is. You truly want to comprehend the deepest qualities of life but not just accept simple explanations. You want to see and experience it all yourself. If you follow your meditation practice with this attitude, you cannot fail. You will find yourself vigilant and being more objective, precisely as things are flowing and transforming from moment-to-moment. Life continues to transform into unbelievable wealth which cannot be described, you must experience it.

The first step in meditation is posture. Posture must be stable and still. You can either be on the floor or on a chair. You can meditate in any place, whenever you feel comfortable. Sit comfortably, with your legs crossed, spread out your fingers (left-cross your right fingers, the two together symbolize method and wisdom) and close your eyes. Quiet your mind and remove any inner and external clutter. Relax your body, especially your shoulders, loosen your arms and legs. Continue to relax the physical body. When you cross your legs and cross your fingers, energy is formed that circulates around your whole body. Eyes are the window of the mind, so your eyes should be closed. All activities of the mind should be stopped. When your body relaxes, energy travels to the next dimension. The mind is nothing, but contains cluttered thoughts that distract your concentration as it thinks of many questions. Continue to observe everything in the mind. Witness your breathing: do not force inhalations and exhalations and let inhalation and exhalation happen naturally. Just be vigilant of your normal breathing. Do not pay attention to thought. Be with your breathing: then the destiny of your thoughts start to fade. When you concentrate on your breathing, negative thoughts cannot enter: you can only concentrate on one object at a time. Eventually your breath becomes smaller and sends a flash between the eyebrows: then you will have no breath and no thought. You will have thoughtlessness. Now your mind is like a clean sheet and you reach the meditation state and can receive blessings from the Universal Source.

Meditation is a method uses to train the mind to acquaint it with high virtue. The more discipline we use to calm our mind, the more peaceful it becomes. When our mind is still, we are free from fear and discomfort and we can attain more joy and happiness. If we can train our mind stay in the infinite present, we shall obtain peace and bliss even in the most adverse conditions, but if our mind is not peaceful, it is difficult for us to attain joy and happiness. Therefore, it is important to practice meditation to train our mind to stay in the moment to attain peace and calmness.

Chapter Sixteen

Fade away

It is understood that all roles on planet Earth are only temporary. Whether it is in Eastern or Western culture, we do not prepare for death while still alive because it something we do not want to discuss and we know we cannot give a quick fix to it or change it. Death is approaching us as we grow older. (Excluding heart attacks or accidental death where death occurs instantaneously.) It is always there in our mind, in our shadows, regardless of our beliefs about what happens after death. Even in the present millennium, we still discuss death less willingly and perhaps we still have a kind of fearful feeling when we meet our final count-down.

Fear of death comes from the unknown, unless we have a near-death experience, as that could calm us and clear away the fear of death. If we have an experience of dying here, then we will be willing to die over and over again, because there is nothing to fear—as each breath ceases, then a new breath is coming in. It is a cycle of birth, old age, illness and death. When one's dead, a new life comes about almost instantaneously. But, while we are still alive, we fear death as it is a mystery: nevertheless we do not like talking about it in a way parallel to discussions about ill-health. We avoid talking about it and view it as abhorrent or bad luck. It is a natural process that no one can deny or avoid, yet we all exist in the same way, whence we come and depart.

Perhaps in the 21st century we will learn that there is no illusion of the fear of death rather by letting it go into the space of emptiness and returning to where we come from in the void, the purity, as the Universe is our home. Then we know there is nothing to be afraid of and begin to relax and believe death can be a joyful event: we are going home to the creator, to be united with the Mind of God.

There are five powerful sources that help us to strengthen our faith in terms of how to live and how to not to be afraid of death, such as determination, adjustment, good quality, blame and inspiration.

When you are aware that your final curtain is approaching, you should do not nothing and believe that there is nothing more you need to do. In fact, there are things you can still do. You prepare everything so that you can go without regret. There are things you must do before you die, then you can die happy.

The moment you find out that you have a year to live, but before your body fades away and your stops working for you, you will get angry, but then something begins to shift, and you begin to unwind: you do not deny it and accept it. You seem to be happier, as if nothing has happened. On the other hand, you can get depressed, upset, worried and get scared, all at the time, and cry with terror: "Oh, no, I do not want it to happen!"

However, you can practice letting go and not letting fear overpower you: you still can lighten up while you are still alive. In fact, we live without struggles against the fact that we are solid and believe nothing lasts forever. Realizing that helps us calm down and can give us much room to breathe and not scream and fight against it. Resistance can cause more fears we do not need, instead of softening everything so we feel calmness and tranquility within. Acceptance is the most important thing to do instead of denying what is real.

What matters is your attitude towards acceptance in facing life and death. For example, an earthquake occurs and everyone hides under the table: but you stand near the window enjoying yourself. Hey! Why are you standing still? You should find refuge! You think whatever happens will happen, there is nothing to worry about and fear. You would rather make a last moment out of it and be yourself and feel the joy within. Well, you may regret it for not trying to take refuge as everyone else does, otherwise you may not still be alive. There are things in our lives we regret having not done and would love to have an opportunity to do again. It is a good idea while we are still healthy and alive to prepare and complete our most important desire, then we can go happy.

When we were younger, we choose the path we walked without regret, but as life progressed we asked ourselves again, "Was I walking on the right path as I am now towards the end of my journey and do I regret the steps which I make now?" or, "I do not feel sorry for what I did and am grateful I lived a full life."

I do not regret what happened in my life, rather I embraced it and thank God for the life I am living now. My early childhood and most of my adult life was not entirely happy. It was not due to family problems, but my own inner sadness and depression. I was born with a genetic disease called Neurofibromatosis that none of the family members have. I resented myself and hated God and confronted Him most of the time because I never understood it. When I reached 47, a profound transformation took place that changed my life to a whole new perceptive: I no longer condemn God, but praise Him for His blessings. I am now working for Him on His behalf and write books through His inspiration. I give all praise and glory to Him because miracles did happen that made me never regret things again. I am grateful for the blessings I have received and will continue to receive. I know nothing will happen to me until I have finished what I have to do on this path, on this journey for His work. By following his guidance, I wrote five books for the benefit of all people across the globe. Yet it all happened in consciousness in the Now. I have no regrets! I miss nothing but feel the peace within.

The most important lesson I learned is that I was healed through awakening to the timeless present. I look forward to doing better and never regret what has happened, as the past is gone while the future is approaching and cannot be validated: the only approach is living in the present moment. There is no pain, no sorrow and no fear, just joy and bliss felt from within. I created my wildest dream and transformed it into reality. I am, I am, I am! I know one day I will have to go, but it will be with no regrets, because I have done something for the highest good of all people. I fulfill my special assignment given to me by God. Again, I have no regrets, but give thanks for everything to the Universal Source, the Mind of God.

How you conduct yourself in your life is always your choice and when that choice is chosen, a decision has been made: you must know what you desire. You can practice five words for how to enhance your life and prepare for your final destination.

When you decide to do something, you carry on until you have finished. You allow nature to guide you so you connect with joy, and relax and have trust. It is a determination to use every tool at your deposal to meet your challenges, as opportunities to open your heart and decide not to give up. One simple way to build this strong determination is to develop a spiritual desire. To do this you can create a role to play. When you wake up in the morning, you can say, "What's happening today, am I going to live or going to die?" You could also say: "What would be, will be. Today is the day I am going to live happily. I am going to live freely and fearlessly. "

Powerful determination gives you all the tools you need to discover yourself and that you possess everything you need: it says that the basic happiness is here, waiting for you to invite in its power to help you to succeed. You have determined not to shut everything down until the whole project is completed and fulfilled.

The next thing is to make adjustments to your life and make room for everything opening to you. You learn how to soften the hardest job on Earth. You learn that you have received everything and stop looking for more needs and desires. Stop saying to yourself, "I need and I want." You develop this through the realization that you are an infinite being: you already have everything you need. You possess two different yous: one with the infinite and one with finite. The infinite side of you has no desire while the finite you has plenty things you need and want. Want and need never end. When you feel desireless, you don't need to search anymore: you return to your real self and are enlightened to the way you want to be: an infinite being with pure energy and emptiness.

You have a seed of higher quality filled with compassion and kindness: you do not need to seek for it anywhere as the power comes from within. All you need to do is trigger the power and it begins to awaken. You just need to relax and perceive clearly what is inside and transform it to the external world and so convert it into joy and happiness.

You confront the gloomy ego. You talk to the ego as, in fact, you are talking to yourself, "You have control over most of my life. I expunge you. I am not listening to you anymore. Be gone, you trouble maker. " This helps you distinguish between ego's thinking and your Inner thought.

Each time you see yourself away from the ego, your mind is void and has no thought. Let it go empty: as you take breath in, you sow new seeds that are able to condition your mind to better thoughts. You may not be able to do it all the time, but the more you try, the more you find that you can do it naturally, without effort. It becomes a habit and, when the mind is emptied, you find out the real you.

You do everything according to inspiration, not from memories. When things are inspired you can do better. You do it with your compassionate heart and kindness. You experience the truth wisdom within that guides you and awakens you to think of others rather than yourself. You feel other pains as much as you think for yourself. It is a way of empowering yourself, not getting what you desire. These five powerful sources will help you if you allow yourself to be empowered by them.

Now pretend that you have six months to live, six months from now you will die. What are the five things you must find out before you die? I said, pretend.

Once we live, then we die. It a natural process and understood: nobody can deny this naked truth. Some people who live life do so with few regrets. Some people live a complete, enriched and joyful life. Others die looking back having missed a great part of their lives, but what does really matter?

What really matters is to find happiness in our lives and enjoy every moment of time on Earth. We want to experience happiness and contentment moment-by-moment and be true to ourselves. But, just having happiness is not good enough: what is missing is finding one's life's purpose. We all have life purposes, some may call it a legacy or that you have left behind something for people to remember you when you were alive. A life purpose is finding life's meaning both internally and externally. We connect with the Inner Source within to attain joy and tranquility and connect horizontally to the external world with people we resonate with in our souls. It is difficult to live alone even when we are not really living by ourselves. We are consciously connected with every soul across the Universe through collective consciousness, but somehow those that resonate with us are all we intent to connect to.

We take this journey only once, we do not know what our next journey will be. Therefore, we must be our true selves and do thing that we want to do so we are missing nothing and have fewer regrets.

It is a good idea to listen to people who have a full life and have found happiness and to learn a thing from them. This is how you find wisdom, when you are willing to talk people and enquire about their experiences and, later on, implement them in your own life. Once thing we realize is that when we reach a desireless state, we feel gratified and do not need to seek anymore. That is true joy and happiness obtained from within. No struggles and no frights occur, because we seek nothing and desire nothing, but we feel peace arising from within and we know what is important to us. You find your true self and be who you are, you live with intention and listen to the Inner Voice and follow your heart.

What will be the things that we regret that we did and hope

that we can reverse before we die? Regret is the most important thing that we fear and we wish that we could go back and do it differently. If death is not what we fear most of the time, then regret is what we really feel deep inside our consciousness when we wish to say to a person, "I am sorry, please forgive me and I love you. Thank you." We complete what needs to be undone through stirring the message up into the air, but regret it when the other person left you with no option. It leaves you with, "I wish I had compensated you for what I had done. I knew I hurt you, but please forgive me. I still love you, my love." If you know you have already tried this, there should be no regrets, just let it go.

You must love yourself before you can cast your love to others. Love is the greatest thing of all and above everything, as feeling that God's love is unconditional. Giving love to others in terms of donating your wealth and professional knowledge and services to help those who need your help, is love. In return, you will receive more love from others who appreciate your help and services. You won't regret it if you have given love and shared your wealth so that people around you can benefit and the world will appreciate you. You will die with no regrets but be full of love that is in your consciousness.

You live in the present moment and feel that happier times will emerge in your life. The present moment is full of hope and expectation and you can do many things in the timeless present. As an infinite being, you create everything in creative consciousness and obtain it through the Universal Source, the Mind of God. The present moment has no fear as you breathe in mindfulness, compassion and kindness and breathe out contentment, joy and blissfulness, stirred into the air and transcended into the invisible black space of the Universe with your positive emotions and vibrations: you connect with the collective consciousness's soul of resonating people and benefit them. You enjoy the present moment and never look back to the departed past and you live happily and die happily. Life is precious and we should enjoy every single moment of our time and try not to miss one moment: when that moment is gone we cannot get it back. When you look into your life, you should always give and let go of everything without reserve, that is really giving. You live a full life with nothing left that needs to be done, then, when the time you need to go comes, you will die a happy man on Earth. You go with a smile on your face.

Finally, death brings fear to your mind because it is the end of a person's life. You fear dead as it is the end, the end of life and the end of enjoying life. We do not want to die because of our hope that we may live happier someday. The future may bring hope that you will live better, even though you may not feel happy about everything in life, but while you are still alive, hope is still there. Yet, when death is near, we should accept rather than reject something we cannot avoid or escape.

If we practice detaching everything and fasten nothing to ourselves, then we are more than willing to accept our faded physical body and not fight with the whole process. Stop struggling against the fact that we thought things could be infinite: in fact nothing is solid and everlasting. Understanding that it can bring peace to our minds and stop us resisting rather than allowing it as real, with gratitude. Death is not the end, but just the end of a faded life and this allows a new breath to enter. It is the end of an old self and the birth of an ever-lasting and ever-evolving spirit that is living forever and lasts infinitely.

Acceptance and Detachment from everything is allowing and giving space for something new to arise and, as soon as one has left, a new life is permitted to enter and bring new hope to the world. Life is a continuum and death is only the end of a cycle: there is no end and no beginning, but just infinity.

Do not let other's fears get on your nerves. Your destiny may not be changed, but it can be a challenge. Everyone is unique and dies as one.

Chapter Seventeen
Kindness and Compassion

When you open your heart to offer your help to others without holding back or keeping anything to yourself, you send out love, kindness and compassion which is not for the goodness of the gloomy ego or collecting merit: then your ego is getting lighter and has vanished into consciousness. The ego is like your dark shadow trying to get through a loophole. If there were more than one Ego, then one of the egos would get through and be irritated by everything that follows. But, when something comes along that does not squeeze and irritate us, we think we can keep it and utilize it for ourselves and benefit from it infinitely. Consequently, we suffer more pains as a result of withholding from ourselves.

The power to change rests within you, even though externally we may be influenced by the Ego and we blame the Ego for all our faults and what we have done to ourselves and others. However, can we blame the Ego for every blunder we committed in the outside world, that spread violence to every corner of the world causing vulnerability to every society and nation?

We have a soft spot that can change our thoughts, emotions and actions by not acting aggressively and violently and instead make peace, embrace love, compassion and kindness. We can also emit truthfulness, endurance, integrity and patience through the warm spiritual heart of Bodhichitta that transcends the energy stirred up into the atmosphere with positive thought emotions, which brings about the vibrational energy that can transform us to become more patient, tolerant, benevolent and kindhearted, and accept each other's differences truthfully with harmony and peace.

These are not delusions or imagination, but optimistic things that can happen to our world that we have inhabited for centuries, but, unfortunately, instead we choose the wrong end of a sword that hurts us and others. The root problems are due to our greed, jealousy and hatred that have been created in the past and wrapped into the present: we just carry on with no intention of settling our conflicts, our hatred, our envy between cultures and nations. The weaker are always taken over by the powerful, as if we were living in the animal world, ruled by the law of the jungle instead of governing by the law of the land.

The truth is that we embrace too much unpleasantness and avoid pleasantness. This ought to be changed if we want enduring peace rather than announcing war between nations, fighting against each other, with or without cause. But, apparently, we have no intention of making any transformational change that makes peace become less difficult, except it may still be possible that hope is still around: only when the time is right, then we will desire it.

If our greatest fear is not death, then what is it that really matters most? Jealousy is one of the fearful and deadly things that most people encounter in their minds. Jealousy occurs because we envy others who possess great wealth and have acquisitions that we lack. We are resentful of others doing better who have accomplished a sea of successes in a relatively short time, plus the comparison makes us feel bad and ashamed of ourselves: we continuously think and believe that it should be happened to us instead of our rivals. The Ego mind always make us feel we are supreme over others. If we cannot do better, then we fail the world: we become a loser and might not stand up among friends and family. You desire to win every time: you go out to challenge the world, even when there is a new challenger arising every day that can bite you, you still feel you are invincible and that you can win because of the pride cast in the Ego mind—you believe you must win or die.

The gloomy Ego mind guides you to try everything on your own accord. To get out of Ego's control, you do not need to look anywhere or attempt seminars, listen to talk, rub your head for answers or seek counsel that costs you a fortune, with no quick fix rather looking deeply within your own consciousness: that would give you free advice without a challenge to your efforts of bagging help without achieving results.

The quick fix is not to ask your neighbors or friends for help: rather, on your own accord, at your own speed, there is a softer approach with no fear, no cost or any unthought-of surprises for you which would make you feel helpless and powerless to resolve your problem. You simply need to stay where you are, acknowledge that you open a window of opportunity from within and you can shut it, but you do not want to do that. It is not that you want to shut it, but you want to make yourself comfortable with this new help until you become gradually familiar with it: then you can let it open and stay active and feel at home that the power has no other agenda other than just emerging to offer you advice and guidance, so you live a loving kindhearted life.

The truth is you are the only one who knows the source is inside you, activated by you and consulted by you. The source within is your invited guest that you use to run everything and puts the mind together to work for you, to protect you from the harsh external world. When you are working with the Inner Source, you no longer need to struggle or fright for life as you prefer swimming with the flow rather than against it. You can remove your protective armor and a thin veil and see the world with your real self. You lighten up and take breaths in with blissful happiness and can continuously connect with the center cord as long as you like, but do not forget to breathe out to complete the practice, and smooth everything out to make you feel positive, to uplift your energy and boost your confidence, enhance your sense of being in the right place at the right time so you meet with right minded people at events that soothe your soul. These can be obtained through the conscious connection with the center cord and only you know that the inner power is right for you.

After test drive of the center cord, you know it is right for you since you feel more mindful, calm and tranquil within and, more importantly, when you feel yourself struggling, you simply let the moment pause to take breaths in and try to find out what's underneath the struggle: if you find yourself complaining, then you know you need to reverse your conscious thoughts to a better energy thought field. Taking breaths in connects you back with the inner cord that guides and protects you unconsciously as distant from the present moment and prevents you from falling into the fluid future without knowing it so you suffer from anxiety attacks.

The reason that we cannot get to our intentions is that we are not in one mind. Our minds cannot serve two masters, only one can dominate the power of the self: that is you. You have no doubt witnessed the self argue within as to who should dominate, but the final say is with you. You decide to choose the Ego or the Inner Source to bless your life. When you choose the Inner Source to navigate your life, gradually you know it is the right decision. Then, you begin to let go of the demanding Ego and it vanishes from your consciousness: you realize you have better control over the rest of yourself. You realize your greater control over anxiety, anger and discontentment and that this is slowly replaced by love, consciousness and feeling the kindness and compassion within arising. You are able to complete the higher aim with the help of the Inner Source and no longer doubt your ability to attain things with self-love; your self-confidence increases tremendously. You begin to embrace the Inner Source that directs your will to the great one, the Mind of God.

Gradually, with your willingness redirected to your desire from within, a new self arises to the surface in you; you no longer need to fight for survival and need to worry no more about weakness; you do not need to cast coins for luck because the whole Universe is behind your back and you abide by the Universal Laws and reach everything that life brings to you.

Sometimes you are willing to look at a thing more deeply because you encourage working with what happens to you instead of blaming others; this is in some way a karmic effect you have had before. Because mindfulness of the Law of cause and effect may get you and you are vigilant in taking precautions and think twice before you take action, you know no blunders occur and you are always consulting your Inner Source for guidance. As a result, with every action you follow your heart and do it right in the moment and it becomes the better choice; every time you do something automatically it transforms you to the conscious present and your whole life feels more relax, more joy and more uplifting experiences than just dreaming. As you are consciously resonating with yourself into a higher power of awareness within yourself, you actually attract happier events into your self-transformed life.

As you continue to get in touch with your heart, you begin to realize that it's vast and infinite. You know how gentle and compassionate this heart is and realize it gets power from the Universal Source, the Mind of God, so immediately you withdraw your fear and doubts. Our world seems less solid and full of illusion and, unlike the spirit realm, it is timeless and limitless. You understand yourself better at a deeper level. You know that you have infinite power, so you can be there for your friends to resolve their troubles if they invite your presence to help them. However, the awareness comes to you automatically when you feel that you can keep your heart open and are conscious that your spirit is present. With the spirit present, you can fulfill everything without effort and be a free spirit.

Finally, when you become a free spirit, you are no longer bound by earthly habits and you do not need to prove anything to anyone, you can simply be and enjoy every moment of your own being present and negative thought emotions cannot enter: as you are in Higher Energy Consciousness, it won't affect your happiness.

Chapter Eighteen
Cheerful Consciousness

When you assess everything that has occurred, now you think of what really matters in your life. Is it really important to find out what you want in your life? No doubt, you realize that after all you live only once, so you desire to discover your life's purpose. Furthermore, you want to feel calm and joyful so you use everything in your power to awaken consciousness in the present moment rather than fall back on the past or forward to the uncertain future that makes you feel uneasy and you do not know how to proceed.

In essence, what really matters is always maintaining a cheerful and joyful mind in the present moment. If you can practice mindfulness, even when you are distracted by the external environment and surroundings, you still uphold a lucid mind and in stillness and silence you perceive everything that arises as energy to awaken you, so you won't fall into unconsciousness under any circumstances or conditions.

However, if you find yourself out of touch and are swept off the wagon into the unconscious scenario, since you practice mindfulness, you are not distracted by the unfamiliar environment and can center yourself and harness your mind by taking breaths during the uncertainty as a way of growing compassion for yourself so you can feel the pains of others as well. Certainly, you can use the distraction to bring yourself back to the now, as after a storm and wind everything returns to the silence, as water makes waves and when waves return they become water unified to become one. Being vigilant, you catch yourself and come back to the conscious present.

Assuredly, when things are returned to silence and get better, that can also serve as a reminder. You continuously stay alert in the moment. Instead of getting delighted and cheerful, you taking breaths out by stirring up the atmosphere with blissful energy transcending the higher vibrations to the Universe so that others can benefit. Since you have shared with the collective consciousness, this allows you to maintain a joyful mind. It also allows you to ease the burden of maintaining your own happiness and the usual load of sad situations and the minor irritations caused by Ego.

On the contrary, one may think that sending out joyful things without holding back to oneself may not be a good idea. A person may agree on the idea of sharing, but giving it all away without keeping some for himself is difficult. That would mean he would not have it at all anymore. Again, he is thinking of a lack. He can gain pleasure and pleasant moments the sooner he unloads the unpleasantness of fear and change the pattern of his thoughts, stopping wanting to resist what's unpleasant and detaching from everything he desires in the mind. Plus, resistance causes the pain; more than anger or envy itself, it's the resistance that causes the pain and suffering. When someone begins to surrender and cheer up, then he realizes non-resistance helps him to relax and open his heart and rejoice.

Now, you relax and apply a non-resistant attitude towards everything and then you realize that you find yourself in a situation where you cannot change the outer environment due to things being out of your control and being decided by a third party. Under these circumstances, you realize it all comes down to your attitude: how you relate to things and whether you continue to struggle against everything that emerges to you or whether you are willing to soften things out in a harmonious way.

Consider this: you can always maintain a joyful mind and that can be helpful in any situation. You continue to lighten up and live life with great bliss. A great happiness arises from the experience and the practice of an empty mind. In fact, we practice breathing exercises in order to be able to relax and cheer up and not take everything that happens too seriously, regardless of our successes or failures, the merits and disadvantages.

The feeling of calmness and bliss in your mind, body and emotions, and a feeling that life is worth living, is due to you no longer holding any resentment deep in your consciousness and replacing it with forgiveness. Sooner or later, you forgive someone that had hurt you in the past: immediately all toxic chemicals flow out of your physical body.

Constantly you eradicate fear, anxiety and anger from your center cord that had suppressed them over the years. Your body begins to heal by the Infinite Healing Energy Presence and any disease that you may have slowly becomes transformed and continuously healed by the Infinite Healing Energy Presence. You forgive everyone and send out love, kindness and compassion to the Universe. You give thanks for the healing that is occurring in consciousness now. You feel worthy of being here; you lighten up and give everything a sense of gratitude and thank the Source. Ultimately, the mind is emptied and, in its natural state, you are totally at ease and rejoice—so does your mind. The finite and the infinite mind are blended so you are now complete. You do not have to experience everything to receive something: let them come to you naturally, and easily. Detachment and gratification is the best incentive to obtain everything including joy and happiness, even though you must feel inner bliss, then start to cheer up. However, you detach from all things, you let the Universe know that you have received something and are ready to receive more and do not feel a lack, therefore, you deserve more. The sooner you receive something, the sooner you share with others so everyone can benefit from your joy and happiness. You feel inner bliss, joy and appreciate everything, including Mother Nature. That's how to click in with joy or bliss. Also, you can look at the sky and say to the Source, "Dear God, I am satisfied with everything I have gotten in my life. Please accept my great gratitude with deep thankfulness. I love you Universe. Thank you." Furthermore, you can go jogging, meditate while walking, or even splash cold water on your face, singing praises to God in a shower—anything that can express your inner bliss and gratefulness. That's how things are enlightened and you feel conscious of a cheerful present.

So, always keep a cheerful and joyful mind even when you are distracted by outside events and circumstances and the best thing that you give to yourself is to feel the cheerful consciousness is present. Let go of things and let the distraction bring you back to the present moment or you can simply walk away and do something different to change the thought pattern. Taking breaths in and out can help you to overcome adverse situations and conditions and bring you back to consciousness in the here and now. (The present is consciousness, the consciousness of the self or reaching life in self-realization. It is the awareness of the shifting moment to the present, thinking of consciousness in the endless now. When you become conscious of the Infinite Self, then the Infinite Self becomes mindful of its presence.) You need to be yourself and create a clear mind within: the connection could be amazing, beyond belief and blossoming.

Chapter Nineteen
Abandon

It is said that if you want to obtain something, then you should detach from it completely: do not think about it, or talk about it, then things will emerge to you in your consciousness to amaze and surprise you. It is as if you wished for something to change and it never got better, so you waited, you were vigilant of your surroundings, then something happened that links you to that consciousness, to that dimension, and you obtained what you desired: it happened almost instantaneously.

However, when you are thinking of making changes in the future, you are actually distant from the present moment. You can never create something that has not yet been created; rather just relax, being present with what you already have or already are. The future dimension is too far away to perceive and predict anything and things can change moment-by-moment: when you think of the future you imagine things. Nevertheless, nothing concrete can be conceived in the moment. When the future approaches, your conditions may have changed your mind, you may get sick or have lost of interest, lost support or the whole environment does not allow you to accomplish your goal. It is an unrealistic goal as long as you have an orientation towards the fluid future, rather bring yourself back to consciousness and satisfy what you have and make it better in the now. You can always keep the thought in your mind but do not push it. When you do well in the present, and the present is wrapped in the future, then you get what you desire. The future has started in the now and the seed of your future is inevitably planted in the present moment. When the future comes, it reflects the potential outcome of things we created and reported back: in reality you are totally ready to harvest in the present. For real success to flow, you only need the right moment and that moment is consciousness.

We find it difficult to stay in the present because we always feel that consciousness now is not good enough to satisfy our demands. Therefore, we take the time machine to travel to the past and hope to find insights from the unreal past and yet we also thought of visiting the unfolded future: even there we may have fears and still be holding onto one hope that it might be a little bit better than the present moment.

Due to some unknown inaccuracy, our time travel machine got stuck and crashed on the rocks: it could not move so we looked out from the window and the sight shocked us. Immediately we perceived many problems and bad memories waiting for us to endorse and embrace them. The problems were more than just bad memories and they hurt us deep within our conscious hearts. We thought those unwanted memories were buried and had been forgiven and forgotten already, but it was untrue. Unfortunately, they recurred out of the blue and flashed in front of our eyes with three-dimensional sounds. "Then", we thought, "Fix the machine! We can travel to the future: perhaps it will give us better insights, perspectives and hope so that our lives can be lived better. We will fix the machine and aim to travel to the year 3003. As soon as the machine landed in the year we desired—hmm huh—we looked at each other's eyes: are we sure this is the future we want to live and the one in which we will find our happiness? We don't belong to the future— their time is far beyond us. They have flying machines everywhere that we do not have in our time. If we live there, it will bring us more problems than we can imagine. Our thoughts and minds have not yet met with their technologies so that makes us anxious to catch up with them. However, if we want to live in the future, we must let the present penetrate the future which allows everything to happen naturally and without pushing it to happen. Everything that occurred has a time sequence and is better to let it happens moment-by-moment, then there is no fear. If we need to wait, than we simply enjoy the present moment and patiently wait for it to come to us. So, we decide to come back to the now and then we understand the present moment is really the best. In the now, we have good health, we have good relationships, we have wealth, we have acquisitions, we have power, and we have gathered merit. In fact, we have everything, but we simply did not give credit for what we are in the present. We are too ambitious and never gratified enough and always desire more for our wants and needs. Sometimes we take on more than we can handle and then we got hurt. Then, we blame the now and think we can do it better in the future. In fact, you do not get it—you use a double edged sword to cast your life, with a sense of things not completely measuring up and all the loose ends will never be tied up. One of the things that keeps us from happiness is continual searching for more pleasure and security—a little bit more of a comfortable situation either at a spiritual or physical level or we look for peace of mind.

The fact is that on the day when we have health problems, quite often we look to different places for help and advice. We try very hard to find answers to fix our wounds and heal our pains. Yet the root of healing is to heal the pain within us and the sooner we heal the pain inside then the sooner the pain will fade. The pain dwells deep within, hurting us to bring us tremendous fear; as a result it causes many diseases to arise such heart attacks, blood vessel blockages, shoulder pains, back problems, cancer, and many other diseases. These problems can be caused by fear, worry and lack of forgiveness and self-love.

One of the major problems most people have today is not being able to forgive others and forget past events and accept that the departed past cannot hurt them again! Those past events were delusional and cannot be validated in consciousness in the now. Anything that cannot be proven to be real is not dynamic, therefore we cannot get fruition. We must go back to the past: confront the past so that you are not afraid of it and are ready to deal with it. You will no longer be imprisoned in the childish feeling that you always need to protect yourself or shield yourself because of the dark shadow behind you. You must accept and agree the dark shadow is departed. You forgive yourself, allowing events to take place, because you are powerfulness and you got hurt, but now you are able to protect yourself fully. You are able to protect yourself even without wearing that protective armor you thought you needed all of the time.

Listen up! Nobody can touch you, even Satan if you do not allow him to comes near you. You have the power to overcome and defeat Satan. You have the power to overcome and defeat your enemy with courage. Your power comes from the source within. It is the source of your own soul that guides and walks with you on your journey. When you get emotional, it is the

Inner Source telling you to slow down and make transformational changes so you can make certain adjustments, change your attitudes toward things in order to enhance your life and then you must move on, living in the Now.

When you live life with a kind heart within, you live with your kind nature that you inhabited from the date you were born. Your kind nature comes with you before you arrive here. As you arrive here, it begins to grow fully as your life evolves and develops and it is always connected with the inner intelligence. It is you who allow it to grow; you live with it fully and allow it to come out to assist you in the harsh world.

When you feel fear, stress, and anger or depression, that fearfulness is the negative side of you: that's the dark angel within and it becomes more active than the light angel. You must make choices and no one can decide for you. It is your show and should be control by you. You are the director and producer and you control the vertical and horizontal. Others are not allowed to decide how you live or run your life. They may give you suggestions on the side, but you are the decision-maker. You are the creator of your own life. You decide to live well or suffer. The choice always rested on you.

In fact, you have many dark angels around, above and below you. When you are afraid, that's the "fearful angel." Each dark angel represents different sides of you and you cannot get rid of them. This is because we are emotional beings and have various states of mind and various moods, going up and down in different life situations. Although you cannot remove them from you, you can keep an open mind and an open heart and eliminate the past: do not admire the future, but let the present be wrapped the future so the future arrives in peace and is rooted very much to the present. When you enter an unconditional relationship with yourself, that means you are aligned with the light angel right now, here in the present.

You continue to live in the present and the present is whatever mood you are in and whatever thoughts are craved in consciousness now.

Chapter Twenty
The Art of Living

The best moment of living is the present moment, the dung of waking up, the manure of achieving enlightenment and the art of living in the now. In fact, it begins with loving kindness for oneself, which in turn is loving compassion for others. We are willing to listen to what others say and see things with our own eyes and implement them in our own lives, utilizing it to work in agreement with what happens rather than continuously struggling alone, feeling helplessness and powerlessness and dragging ourselves down.

This person drags himself down to depression because he won't listen and walks on his own path. He was abused by his mother in his childhood and hurt badly and deeply. He suppressed his hurtful feelings within without letting them out. Growing up into adulthood, he got married and raised two intelligent children with plenty of hope and expectations. Unfortunately, when he reaches his mid-forties, due to losing his professional career, he began to drag himself into chronic depression and his past memories came back to hunt him. He shut himself off, seeing nobody, and, worst of all, was not willing to listen or seek help. Then, recently his high blood pressure reached a sky-high and dangerous level. Is this the way that we want to live our lives? Why do we act so selfishly, without thought, torturing ourselves and at the same time our foolishness affects and hurts those around us. Why do we allow our finished past to come back to hurt us? We have a choice: nothing can come to us without our invitation. The hurtful past stored in subconscious mind can be cleaned out. We have the power to control what sort of thoughts can emerge to us. That negative emotional thoughts enter the mind is a warning sign that urges us to make transformational changes before we really get hurt. However, when you get emotions, it is the Inner Self feeling upset, trying to give you a signal to improve yourself instead of continuing to sleep on the sleeper train without waking up. The Inner Self tries to wake you up before it is too late. Most of the time we do not listen to the power within, then we regret that it is too late—or not too late only when we listen. It is sad to see a person destroy himself and torture his own family because he allowed the past to hunt him and he continued living in the past instead of living in the now. He is like a lonely wolf living in a jungle feeling very lonely, feeling nobody wants him and is just waiting to be called. I understand this person wants to catch the attention of others, but he was acting from the wrong direction. Why did he insist on seeking attention from those who do not value and love him? He has a lovely wife and two wonderful smart children who love him dearly. Does he not think it is good enough or is it because his Ego wants to be recognized by those who repel him? His case is similar to ones everywhere across the globe. He will continuously sleep on a sleeper train and does not want to wake up. Perhaps his false mind reminds him that if he wakes in the now he feels more pain and sorrow. Only when you have been there do you know what it feels like and therefore you can do something that you hope will open the space and cause things to keep flowing instead of being motionless. You can help someone to be connected with their own insight with boldness and gentleness, and see them make improvements in their conditions and circumstances.

Dragging all the blame to others comes from the fact that we have been hurt and therefore we want to hurt back. Therefore, we think it is logical to return our hurtful feelings to others so they have a taste of how we feel when hurt. It is a wrong, illogical and bad thought. You give your power away by torturing yourself while others do not know about it or care for it. Instead, you should move on: forget about the painful past that you cannot undo. The whole dilemma is not just about you. It is about whether you care that those who love you will get hurt because of your willful actions and negative emotional thoughts: you can never change those who injured you. You must be honest to yourself and open your heart and accept who you are cannot be changed, but you can remove your pains and begin to live anew in the now.

Yet, you can have any kind of life you desire because it is your life. However, do you live a joyful, happy and purposeful life right now? What is pain? What is fear? What is chronic depression, really? They all dwelt in your Ego mind comfortably, and refuse to leave you until you determine to eradicate them out and turn your adverse conditions into a healthy fearless life and live in the timeless now. The Ego mind loves to see you get hurt so it has more command over your life. The Ego is like a wild horse: you need to tame it so you gain control of the beast and transform the Ego mind so it combines with the subconscious mind into one consciousness in the infinite now.

Some people are very cautious about their lives and even use negative emotions, limitations, failures, illness and pain as a form transforming and learning lessons. It taught them to let go of a false-self and be unimpeded by Ego-dictated goals and desires. It gave them a depth of compassion and kindness and they sent that out to the world and it made them more real.

Whatever happens to you, there is a deep spiritual cause, even a short-term illness or an accident can show you what is real and unreal in your life, what does matter and what does not. Your Inner Self wants you to change for the better to live a better quality of life. It seems that when you stay in the higher prospective, you always feel positive. In fact, they are as they are and when you live in complete acceptance of what is—you begin to live comfortably and there is no good or bad life but simply being. The good or bad life is always there, balanced out the imbalance or the lack, and all perspectives in our mind.

You are not pretending the bad conditions are good, you accept them as they are. You allow it to be like this to prevent the mind from resisting it and creating more negative patterns. It is part of the essential healing progress and an important aspect of forgiveness.

Forgiveness of the past is only a portion of it: additionally you need to show forgiveness in the present and clean the present moment. If you constantly clean the present moment and allow it to be as is, then eventually there will be no negative ingredients accumulated and no resentment can be felt that needs to be forgiven, as the future penetrates the present so all emotions are vibrated as positive thoughts that have been cleaned.

Furthermore, forgiveness is a wild card: it can cover everything you want to forgive in order to reduce sadness, unhappiness and grief, but, provided that you have relinquished resistance, underneath the sorrow and grief you find calmness, tranquility and stillness, conscious of God's presence and conscious of thought. The omnipresence of God will wash out all pains and suffering and enable you to endure every situation and turn it into transformative peace and harmony.

Although we may accept our life cannot change, the present is changing from moment to moment: as situations change, your condition will shift transmuting to the better so you feel good within. When you feel good, it will give you a positive transformative effect. Therefore, you must be vigilant of your surroundings and ready to modify to what could more suitably meet your needs.

Apparently, some people need to experience a huge amount of pain before they will awaken and accept, and before they will forgive. As soon as they do, they begin to experience the awakening of Self-realization conscious of what is evil, the transformation of suffering into inner calmness and peace. Eventually, what we perceive as evil from our imperfect perspective could be used as part of a reflection on the highest good that has no negative. However, you must accept through forgiveness. Except that you make it happen, evil has not been tamed and remains in control and, therefore, there is no change.

Through forgiveness, you no longer carry the burden of the past and allow the present moment to be as it is, and then miraculous exchanges happen, not only internally but also transcended to the external world. Your have entered a state of silence, both within and without you. Your changes can be seen, what is visible will appear sometime in the latter day. Your pain is now dissolved and healed, you dispel the unconsciousness automatically simply by holding the radiance of consciousness as present.

Most of the time unwanted things that happen to people's

live are due to unconsciousness. They are self-created. When you are fully alert, these incidents do not come into your life anymore. The Ego runs your life when you are not present or in the state of unconsciousness, unable to observe thoughts entering the mind. The Ego considers itself a separate entity with no concrete inner consciousness with any other being. The Ego treats other beings as war-time rivals, it sees them as a potential enemies. The Ego's thoughts of everything are limited and insufficient and fight their own battle. An Ego-centered mind and the Ego's behavior are greed, resistance, envy, power, defense, and attack. The Ego's strategies are clever, but it has never solved any of its problems. The answer is so simple: the Ego itself is the trouble.

When many egos come together, whether in a relationship or in business, bad things happen such as conflict, power struggles, violence, and chaos. This includes war, disorder and mayhem caused by massive unconsciousness in some particular region, or in some country, which is controlled by a tyrant. In addition, ill-health and many different types of disease arise which are also caused by the Ego's continuous resistance, which create limitations and cause blockages in the flow of energy through the body. Only when you are realigned with the Inner Source and are no longer controlled by your Ego mind do you stop creating those aggressive things. Therefore, you do not practice the play anymore.

Whenever there are egos together, drama of one kind is guaranteed. Even when you are alone by yourself, you will create your own play. When you did something wrong and feel regret, that's a tragedy. When you deliberately allow yourself to revisit your unwanted past and let the past take over the present, you are creating time, psychological time—the thing out of which a play is created. Whenever you dishonor the consciousness present by allowing it to be chosen, you are creating a stage show.

When you have completely accepted the life you have, that is the end of all the Ego's control. The fact is, nobody can tell you how to run your life. They cannot argue with you: even if you want to sleep with evil, it is your own choice. It is hard for others try to change you, unless you agree to change of your own accord. However, when you are fully conscious and know what you are doing is for your greatest good, then there is no real conflict and you do not need to explain, to defend or attack. So, there won't be any disaster. No one in a lucid state of mind can create conflict. Your mind is clear, there is no conflict within you or the conscious mind. You and the mind have the same expectation; therefore you do not need to do anything to experience everything.

Life begins from within and is infinite, timeless and formless, while physical form is only temporary, an illusion and unreal. Your beautiful external self is not real: in time it will age and fade away. Your external self makes you happy and unhappy. When you connect yourself to the formless self within, you can watch and allow your external self grow old from a place of tranquility and peace. Since you have observed the aging progress from within, when your physical appearance fades, it becomes unimportant and expected that you let its beauty shine from within and reflect the external self. In fact, your external beauty is not faded, rather it transforms into a spiritual form of reflection. Let your inner beauty continue to shine on you and transcend the best out of you and let it all go out to the world and benefit all. That is the beauty of a true Being—beauty from within.

Life contains pleasant and unpleasant moments, in addition to suffering or gratification, it is all in one basket. We think it is separated: in fact, there is no separation. It is separate through the illusion of time. If we recognize the prophetic words: *everything happened for a reason and nothing will last forever* then we will understand: *there is a time for richness and a time for not encouraging* in our lives and at the end nobody wins it all. What we perceive as negative is a warning signal to encourage us to make transformational changes to clean the poisons from our minds and the body so that, later, we can do better so we do not carry the illusion on forever and we do not allow it to follow our lives. In fact, good things or bad things are a sequence: as we seek them there is always enjoyment, and no pain or suffering. We simply walk through what nature has prepared for us. Then we will appreciate every moment is a seed of adventure that is guided by the hands of invisible forces encouraging us to see through to what's underneath all our behavior, such as thought emotions, hatred, anger, and envy. We acted them out repeatedly. We practice mindfulness, and put all these negative ingredients in one basket including the gloomy Ego. Gradually, our clinging onto the Ego will be weakened and the kind heart will emerge in consciousness. We make friends with the Ego and then shut it off and let the compassionate heart observe and harness our body and mind and know we do not have to be afraid of anything: at the end all be well and looked after.

Whatever we seek in the material world can never gratify our wants and needs, yet we never give up looking for things that can bring us happiness and enjoyment. But, somehow, the more intention we have of seeking happiness, the more we won't get it. Nothing in the external world can satisfy our unlimited wants and desires, except only give us temporary adjustments to the illusion of pleasure, but you need to pass through many unreal experiences before you recognize that truth. Everything you seek will get results, but it will also give you pain. Things will give you pleasure, but not joy. Pleasure gives you a feeling of delight or gratification or something that is satisfying, and it is different from joy. Joy arises from within the spiritual self. The inner peace that you feel is only found in the inner state of peace that is the presence of God. It simply arises naturally without you seeking or asking for it. You do not need to struggle to attain it, but simply be mindful and express it from within.

The joy and love of God is your refuge and restful end: you know something so precious so real and ever-lasting is deep in the center cord of your Being. You could not find it anywhere, but you feel the joy in the center of your heart in your natural state of consciousness in the here and now. You allow and accept the present moment to be and permit and desire the temporary nature of all things and conditions. Thus, have you found joy and inner peace.

Accepting and offering no resistance to life enables you to be in a state of grace, and lightness. This state is no longer dependant on material things that would give you pleasure or make you regard things as bad or good. You are not dependant on the external environment and the inner self-dependency on structure or shape vanishes. There is no form, but emptiness. You see that you are spirit. You are free from all things and feel the void and emptiness. The external form of your life improves tremendously: people, events, circumstances and things come to you effortlessly and you are free to accept or reject them, and appreciate all. These events, people and conditions will still be in a circle of coming and going, but your dependency is less. There is no fear to be felt, but life continues to flow with simplicity.

The happiness that is reliant on material things in the external world never lasts. It is all delusional and a pale reflection of the physical self. The vibration you find from within is true happiness, when you enter in the moment of non-resistance. Living infinitely takes you beyond the physical mind so you can comprehend and be liberated from things. Even the environment is not so encouraging as to make you crumble, but you would still feel a deep inner tranquility and serenity attached. Perhaps you are not so happy in the moment, yet the silence and peacefulness is still with you. You are at peace.

Chapter Twenty One
Surrender all

Here surrender means letting in God or letting go of something beyond your control, your power and resistance. It does not mean you are being defeated or giving up, failing to succeed in life, but a pure form of letting go in your life gives it over to the capable hands of the invisible Universal Source, the Mind of God. Letting go does not mean you are being passive and doing nothing for your life, rather you are more active with a positive attitude to life, and consistently look for exits, but it is non-resistant approach, it does not irritate situations further to make it more difficult to fix. You are simply following the flow of life in the now and accepting the present moment unconditionally without keeping anything. There is an inner and outer conflict whether to relinquish to what is, or whether there is a loophole between the demands and expectations of your conscious mind and what is. Life does not always embrace you when things go wrong: you surrender to what is and transcend from the circumstances and accept something you cannot change: you free your mind from challenges and you are thus realigned with the Inner Source. Resistance occurs only in the mind. When there is no mind, the mind is thoughtlessness, then pain is eradicated and all negativity vanishes into the thin air and your overall conditions continue to improve in the timeless now.

For example, if you were stuck in flowing sand in the Sahara desert, you won't say, "I accept I am stuck in the mud and surrender." It is wrong and a misunderstanding of the true meaning of "surrender". Letting go does not mean you sit down and hope something will emerge to remove you from harm's way. You should actively look for exits to withdraw yourself from danger: concentrate on resolving it in the present moment. You do not flight or judge what has happened, but narrow your attention down to the now without prejudice and accept you could not change what has happened. Therefore, there are no negative emotions felt in the mind. Then, you accept that you are stuck in the mud: it is real and you are constantly trying to get yourself out of the mud. That is a positive approach rather than condemning yourself with negative attitudes, which arise out of anger or frustration: that won't secure you from further disaster or will worsen the situation without solution. You surrender to your conscious present and a lucid mind will get you out of danger.

On the contrary, non-surrender makes the situation harder and makes the Ego consciousness present and separates you from mindfulness presence. Your surroundings and the people around you become an immediate threat, as you perceive it in the mind. You treat people around you as your enemy, you judge them for no concrete reason and your perception and interpretations are dominated by fear and caused by impairment in your mental imbalance of distrust: a dysfunctional fearful state of consciousness.

Furthermore, it is not only your psychological form and its

impairment that can affect you: your physical body becomes rigid and stiff through resistance. Stiffness could occur in different parts of your body and block the free flow energy through the body, the healthy functioning of the body is influenced and restricted. Body restriction can be resolved through physical therapy or meditation, it can be helpful to restore the energy flow temporarily, but in the long run you need to practice surrendering in consciousness in the timeless present: that is the way to permanent release and dissolves the pattern of resistance. The past can no longer change while the future is unfolded in the current moment, emerging in the now. The trouble that created these situations in your life can only be resolved by your power to and broken through surrender, and you held the key to unlock the portal of your life. It is your life, your Infinite Self which exists in the eternal realm of the spiritual world in the infinite present. The conscious infinite life presence is all you that need.

It is absolutely fine to take action and even initiate change to attain your goals. But, surrender reconnects you with the Source energy of your Infinite Self: if what you are doing is inspired by the Infinite Self, it will turn out to be a joyful celebration of life's flow of energy that will guide you deeper into the present moment. Through relinquishing the quality of your mindfulness, as a result of what you are doing or have created, all is enhanced amazingly. The results will then take care of themselves and reflect that quality. It is the significance of awareness at this moment that is the major determination of what kind of future you will experience, so to relinquish is the most important thing you can do to attain positive transformation. Action is not primary, but surrender can transcend it. Any positive action cannot be achieved with an opposed state of consciousness.

The sooner you surrender, the sooner you will see clearly what you have to do to transform the situation: you may do one thing at a time, that is fine. You must stay focused on each thing. Have vigilance over the changes of nature: see how everything is transformed from seeds growing and evolving to a flower with little or no effort and how life unfolds into consciousness and that brings gratification or happiness. Nature transforms by itself and through surrender to what is. That is the power of surrender: there is a guiding force that guides you to what you need to do to open your mindfulness; then cease to be harnessed by external circumstances. You no longer need to resist, and the light helps you cut through the uncertainty of unawareness. You can do everything to improve your life: all actions will be inspired, but act on one thing at a time so you won't be confused and so get it right. You continue to project your actions in the now. Do not worry if you cannot get results immediately, but be patient and anything you do must not be done in resistance. Furthermore, if you cannot take any action, you should simply stay still, surrender deeply in consciousness now and ensure you are aligned with your Inner Self. When you enter the present, change can take place from moment-to-moment effortlessly on your part. Life will be easier and more helpful if you go with the flow and are cooperative. No inner obstacle can emerge to prevent you from taking action, because you are guided by the light of your own conscious presence and are mindful.

You surrender to the Inner Self of your own Infinite being without condition. You surrender your life to the Inner Source that transcends your life so you live the quality of life you want. Illness is part of your life's situation that you cannot avoid. It consists of the past and the future. It brings it forward and will continue until you are living in consciousness now. There are various reasons for your condition which exist in the past and are wrapped into the present, but within you there is an Infinite Self that can help you to remove your illness in the timeless present, when you activate it.

When you discover your illness, if you continuously focus on it, then it will transform into more pain, mental illness and further transform into a heart condition or physical disability. However, if it is a serious health issue, you must take steadfast action to seek medical advice in consciousness Now, to fix the problem instantly and quickly. You must not surrender to the illness, but allow yourself to surrender into the present moment into the state of awareness by looking into the cause of karma, and then you awaken to the cause of your illness. It opens your mind to enlightenment and makes transformational changes immediately. Surrender does not transform what happened, but it transforms you. When you are transformed, your surroundings are transformed because the environment is only a reflection of you.

On the other hand, illness or sickness is not a problem: indeed, you are the problem. It is you, who cause the illness in your physical body. No illness can emerge in you without your agreement, but do not feel guilty or blame yourself. It will make your illness worsen: rather accept and surrender to what is without further resistant. Mirror your illness to good health and constantly believe you will get well soon. Do not fall back on the past or future, simply focus on the present moment and remove time from your illness. You must focus on the present moment and things will transform. Do not get angry, or feel pity about your illness, but mirror it and use it with spiritual awakening and regain self-realization and surrender that brings to an end the Ego mind's control that pretends to be you, the "false self."

See if you awaken in the conscious present and transmute illness into good health and suffering into the achievement of a spiritual state. You tame the Ego and accept illness is a part of the healing transformation and not your true Infinite Self. Your Infinite Self will not get sick, as sickness only occurs in your physical body: nevertheless your Infinite Self will temporarily be affected. Your Infinite Self is an emotional being. You and the Infinite Self are one source, blended to walk on the same journey here. However, your illness does not reflect your true eternal self, as who you really are. You are always identified as an Infinite Being in the timeless present.

If our lives always have choice, why do we enter the same old condition over and over again without being mindful that we are on the wrong path? Before we decide to do something, everything is just an illusion: nothing is created. We have the power to choose which strategies or stimulus is right for us and then we make our final decision and take appropriate action, and subsequently transform the action into a physical form in the external world as our reality. However, choice indicates that we are conscious of what we do in the moment when the decision is made. Without being attentive to your decision, you have no choice. In other words, you defy or transcend the mind that you have chosen to do something consciously present in the now. Your spiritual present allows you to make that steadfast decision and does not recognize the mind and make decisions in the timeless now while the mind still in time. That means you have jumped steps without stopping to think, feel or act in certain surroundings according to the conditioning of the mind. However, if you stop trying to think, crave emotions and do it in certain ways and identify with the mind, then the mind will guide you back to the same old pattern that you were in previously, the one that the mind feels comfortable in, so it can stay in time. You stay completely unconscious and identify with your mind. In fact, it does not matter whether you are intelligent or highly educated, when you are unconscious, you still will fall and agree with the mind and so do foolish things: as a result, you cause disaster or unhappiness in your life. Therefore, you must make yourself balanced in everything and inevitably mindful of your current conditions: do not let the mind set your life and become your master: that would avoid the potential of sadness, suffering and adversity occurring in your life.

You always have a choice about all things, unless you choose not to exercise your right and unconsciously let the mind recreate the familiar old program that you experienced in the past. Even though it is painful, it is known to the mind. The unknown is not secure, because the mind has no control over it and understands it, despite the fact it is not recognizable. That is the reason the mind dislikes the timeless present. The mind does not like the present moment, since it creates a loophole not only in the mind but also in a continuum of space between the past and future. Without slipping into that empty space, nothing new can enter this world. It is through that gap that the infinite present becomes possible. The gap can be described, as you have a thought and then a second thought, there is a gap between your first and second thoughts. Therefore, through the gap between thoughts, you stop to think and clear the mind to allow the infinite present.

Now let's go back to the question, why do we choose to repeat the old patterns or faults over and over again? The reason is that you recognize with the mind a pattern created in the past that is not separable. It could be influenced by the negative experiences created in the past that you do not deserve to have a good life, or you deserve to be punished for some reason that is stuck in the mind. Perhaps you have suffered enormous pain in your childhood, so automatically you seek more pain unconsciously. But, this is only an excuse, or a self-created situation. It is the mental emotion that was created in the past, but change can be made by overriding the past and moving to the present moment. You can always crave your thoughts in consciousness in the present and free yourself from the invalid past and meditate on inner self-mindfulness. Only when you act in consciousness now is there no pain and you break through your unwanted condition, that choice is timeless now.

We all deserve to live a comfortable and abundant life and nobody intentionally chooses to live a dysfunctional life to put themselves in a harm's way. It happens because you are unaware of the conscious present to dissolve the past, and are not powerful enough to fight the evil. You are not fully conscious of what you do. You still are sleeping on the sleeper car in the train. Meantime, the gloomy Ego mind is harnesses your current condition and is observing your life.

As long as your mind is running your life, then your choice is temporarily suspended and turns into an illusion because you are not in the conscious present and, if you are not here, what choice do you have? Think about it.

We all suffering from illness, up to some point. The moment you recognize your illness, you substitute it for compassion and love. You recondition it with kindness for your physical body, so that you will not create further suffering and pain. Until you clear the burden of illness in your pained body, the awareness of your conscious present is dimmed and pushes you out of the conscious state. However, there is always something you can do to yourself to transcend your condition with forgiveness. You can truly forgive yourself by totally eradicating and terminating your connection with the past. You use your infinite power to forgive yourself because the infinite is always conscious in the present. Only the eternal now has the power to release you from the past and make the past powerless. You recognize your power is the infinite present and therefore no power can compromise you as an infinite being and you know who you truly are. Then, you do not even need to ask for forgiveness because the infinite in the eternal now can and will observe everything and all things are forgiven.

Finally, when you surrender to the conscious present, the invalid past is powerless. You know you do not need it. Living in the conscious present gives the power to live abundantly, fearlessly and a healthy life. Only the conscious present is the answer to your timeless present and eternal life.

Chapter Twenty Two
Communication from the Inner Self

When you suffer from painful experiences, you want to cease communication with everyone because it hurts, but have you ever considered moving closer to that experience? The reason to get closer to that pain experience is that you can clear that condition, knowing that it cannot hurt you anymore, so you can live painlessly and fearlessly in the present.

One specific action you can take to soften your pains is to communicate with the Inner Self. When you speak with your Inner Self, you speak aloud so your vibrations can transcend into the Universe with one intention, that others can hear you. Then, you observe if you receive any response from the collective consciousness. You may get an answer from others if you allow the response to enter the mind: that may help to ease your pain.

You should always consider meditating on whatever arouses resentment. You use it as a reminder. When you feel restless, afraid, and hopeless, it is a reminder to listen and hear the voice from within.

When you feel resentment about the words that we speak, the thoughts that we have and the actions that we undertake, they are not manifestations of the effects that we were hoping for. Beyond that, we are so aggressive we are not adding any peace to people around us and the world. Resentment reminds us not to feel sorry for ourselves, but to open up more to the pain and dwell in consciousness in the present moment.

If we want to connect to the Inner Source within, we need to give up our pride, be meek, discard knowing what to do and surrender everything to the inner power. When we communicate within, we relinquish our agendas as they block us from seeing the entity before us. We allow the Inner Spirit to guide us where we need to be.

When you communicate with the spirit inside, you must use your thoughts, your words, and your emotions to convince yourself how desperate you are to seek its help. Alternatively, everything you say, do and think can support your keenness to communicate, to move closer and trust that the spirit can offer help and you are not separated from the Source.

Now we open communication with the spirit by listening to what the spirit has said to us. You told the spirit how you feel about your adverse conditions and situations, then you just patiently wait. Then, in silence, you hear and sense an answer from the spirit saying, "I want to see if you can convince me to do it your way."

Communication is a challenge to us, if we learn how to communicate with others. It is not only that we can help meet our needs in consciousness, but we can also help others to meet their needs. It helps us to see what the meaning of communication is and understand each other's differences so we make transformational changes, become less aggressive towards everything including how we treat the Mother Nature, and live peacefully and serenely on this planet.

We are unique: the uniqueness allows us do things independently and freely. One person's idea of trash may be other person's treasure. What you may regard as important may not be important to another. You may think your idea is brilliant and out of this world, but the investor may not think so. Hence, this shows that we are all different and we have to accept and recognize that. So, instead of abhorrence and not enduring each other and, at the extreme, going to war, let's hold the Winter Olympics. Let's settle our differences in gamed instead of using weapons, guns and bullets and sending fighters to each other's territory and destroying each other. Through games, we can play in harmony with each other and play together, even though we are on opposite teams. Winning or losing is not important, but simply playing the game. Play to play. Through playing games, we settle our differences and clear our conflicts in the game instead of leading us to war or the destruction of the planet.

One of our problems is that we never give in and refuse to step aside so that the other can loosen up and try to achieve harmony and smooth everything out. The point is to live together on this planet Earth with our differences, to communicate for our own stakes. The process will take a long time, we do not even know when to reap results. If we want to achieve our peace, but we all put guns on the table with aggressive tactics, then can we expect change or are we able to accomplish good results?

In fact, it is not true that we cannot communicate, but we all hold our opinions in our minds and label others through bias before we connect and are willing to talk. However, if we can really see each other's differences and do not try to change them and just accept and see them, that's how things begin to change. We can always apply breathing in and breathing out and begin to connect the world without resentment, prejudice, and judgment. Powerful communication is sending kindness and compassion out from our compassionate heart. If we all do that, a global incentive for peace becomes possible. An important thing we can do to prevent conflict or labor wars is to stop talking about how we perceive and predict WWIII will happen. If we keep talking about WWIII, then one day it will just break out and all the human race will be destroyed by one crazy tyrant's decision to use the atomic bomb and then… Surely, we do not want this to happen? Then we must stop talking about it, rather predict peace or attain the incentive for global peace. Then, the whole global condition will change and improve. Is it not peace that we all want?

This important thing is you should extend peaceful practice to everyone, not excluding anyone. When we stumble upon life in a dangerous situation then our compassionate heart is activated, we breathe in pain in the circumstance that confronts us and breathe out thoughts that will help. It's definitely fine to breathe in pain and breathe out compassion, relief and love. The true meaning of compassion is that everybody needs someone to be there for them, just be there.

This person was seriously injured after a car accident and her appearance was disfigured: even though plastic surgery helped to improve her looks a little, it was difficult to endure her life. It affected how the harsh world perceived her. In this insensitive world we are judging person on her appearance. We always look at the outer appearance of a person. In fact, the external self is just a shell, and in time it will grow old, only the Inner Self lasts infinitely. But, this person was lucky enough to have some good-hearted people look after her. These volunteers came to visit her and talk to her. They did not know what to say, but were simply there to support her spirit so she could get through psychological hard times. In difficult times, we all need to have someone around us so that we won't be alone. Mental, psychological, and spiritual support are vital to boost our recovery from illness or any perceivable problems. Support from another person is such that sometimes we do not need to say anything. The most important communication of all is just to be there to show you care.

We can also extend our compassions to different situations and let it arise naturally without bias, and then move to our enemies. Here "enemy" may mean people who do not resonate with your soul, and it does not necessarily mean "enemy in the combat zone". Perhaps we should not label it. To label others as the enemy causes negative emotions, hatred and anger and is not advised. So, you need to clean it from your subconscious mind. You want to send out compassion, kindness and love to others and you should do it without bias and prejudice and judgment. Your compassionate heart does not distinguish between people and treats everybody equally. You start where you are, whatever you feel, you send out a wider angle of compassion so everyone benefits.

Sending out kindhearted energy may not occur spontaneously; sometimes you need to be inspired to make it happen. It is not something you can fake, but a little encouragement is needed. Most of the time you know when you are inspired by the Source that arises in the moment, then you sent out the energy. Since you do not defy anyone, maybe you can practice during meditation to try to see what happens when people you dislike are standing in front of you or intentionally bringing out the memory of a person you disliked: breathe out compassionate energy in meditation sessions. Create a visual image in the mind that you try to communicate with the person you dislike. What would you say to him or her? What would it take for you to be able to hear what he or she is trying to say to you? It is communicated through your heart via meditation. Do not distinguish or label others as people you like or dislike and practice everything with no separation. When you connect with your own pains, reflect that others are able to feel in consciousness exactly what you feel. Their pains may be different from yours. When you practice long enough, you notice your Inner Self, and when all other Universal collected conscious minds are connected, then you begin to realize that the Inner Self and other collective consciousnesses are actually no different.

Chapter Twenty Three
Reality

What is real and what is unreal? If the real and unreal are only imaginary in our minds, then there will be no difference between what we see as physical and as an illusion. In fact, real and unreal are not separable at the bottom line: when a story is told thousand times, then we believe it, transforming the impossible become our own truth.

When we find ourselves in the same undesired drama playing again and again, usually we want to escape, but we crash at the wall; sometimes we think we must be cursed. Is that real too? It is absolutely untrue to believe that you are under a spell. Without feeling emotions cultivates in the mind, it is difficult to create miserable dramas to frighten yourself as if you were in a big crisis. God will not allow this to happen to you. If you believe in being cursed, basically you are saying that the Source has not done its job to protect you. You know that the Universal Source always protected and loved you. The only person that can curse you is "you" through your own thoughts, words and actions. So, perhaps you should not impose any negative emotional energy on yourself and at best practice living in consciousness in the now. In fact, what you cast into your life is what will return to you. If you continue to cast any unreal dramas into your life, what you wish for will be granted. Life is what you put into it.

Sometimes we are caught in a situation we feel is impossible to get out of or that it is impossible to give in. Then, you think you should squeeze yourself out through a gap and apply a softer approach to the root of the problem and, at the same time, you have received a vision. That is interesting as it softens you and you receive the big perspective. Perhaps that softer approach humbles you so that it transforms everything constantly allowing you to accept the thing for what it is and so you do not struggle or challenge it anymore. You relinquish, then, your soul guides: you walk on the right path to melt away your troubles.

However, there are dilemmas created by a third party or a rumor brought to you through media-mongers: you do not need to believe it unless you can validate it. Buddha said, "Do not believe a word of what others have said, even I said it. You must prove it yourself before you take it in and trust it."

There are disturbed rumors saying the world will end on December 21st, 2012. If you wait for the world's end, then you will be awfully disappointed because it will not happen. The difficulties come from the emotions stored in our minds concerning the Mayan Prophecy. Do you believe it? It is unreal and untrue: it is only fear craved into your mind, then, if you believe in it, it will become your own fearful reality. Besides, it is only a prophecy for the future and is nothing concrete or built on rock, declaring for sure it will happen. If we believe that nonsense then we are not living in real time. It is as if we go back to the date before the year 2000: tales said that all computers will crash because computers were not set and ready. These rumors were proved invalid, but an enormous number of people in that industry gained vast financial means as a result. If we allow rumors to get into our nervous system, we certainly will get scared, because they create emotional fear and guide us far from the present moment in the now, which has no peace and tranquility but fear. The mind loves to reside in the future which has time and can bring you more emotional fear and vulnerable anxiety and painful expectation, because the future is unpredictable and unknown. We need to learn to live in the now, and not the past or the fluid future, which has not yet unfolded. Only when we disbelieve what is right now, right at this conscious moment, then when the future rolls over, it just another moment: furthermore, how stupid it appears, when the year December 21, 2012 approaches, it transforms into just another day, without fail, and is lived and we move on.

The year 2012 will not bring the world to an end, rather it will be the opening of a new spiritual age. Now, while we are patiently waiting for the future to approach, we need to stay awake, be alert and mindful and let the future arrive naturally. In the meantime while we are waiting for the future to emerge, we just need be ourselves and enjoy ourselves in the conscious moment and let loveliness and peacefulness arises in the motionless of our presence.

People who spread this kind of fearful rumor to mislead others have one purpose in mind, which is to gain money, reputation and fame. The world will not come to an end as predicted by the Mayans or I'Ching. No one knows when the world will end. The God who created us will not let us dismount without difficulties. Why people get so obsessed about WWIII and the end of the world is beyond our understanding. Can we perceive something better, rather than war or the end of the world? Perhaps our conscious mind likes to create the fear, chaos and discontentment that we perceive within, as we project out, and they become our ultimate fear illusions. We perceive the illusionary world will never have a peaceful end because we are not living in consciousness in the now. We always like to predict something that is happening in the future and then, when the upcoming date approaches, it turns out to be unreal: then we predict it again and again and never stop predicting our future. The problem is the prediction is never positive: rather, we love to predict war dramas or that the end is coming. Why do we want this kind of drama? Do we not see the world has enough chaos and despair already? We need to be clear and lucid in our minds and stop craving or predicting negative events that may or may not occur in the future, but live in the moment with harmony and calmness. Then many positive things will arise in our world via peace, stillness and serenity.

Today the stress is on how we avoid this unwanted desire craved into our mind: the answer is to filter them constantly and be vigilant for any emotional thoughts penetrating the mind, so we are inevitably aware of our thoughts. We need to keep our hearts open allow the compassion, kindness and love to squeeze in. We should not crave hopeless thoughts and continue to be calm and be patient. Patience means allowing things to unfold in their own sequence, rather than jumping in with our own usual responses to fear or terror. Patience allows us to clear our minds so that everything is harmonious and goes well. Patience allow you to think about what you hear and see and allows you time to analyze, prove whether unfolding future events are not genuine: you have a choice to believe them or cast them out. Patience implies a willingness to see an event as it unfolds, rather than trying to seek to validate it. Since you cannot prove anything that has not yet happened, rather note it, stay calm and feel the silence within: let the moment guide you and benefit from the conscious moment. Take a deep breath and see yourself surrounded by the Divine Light and your body filled up, and feel God's consciousness within you. Stop thinking of anything and pay attention to the conscious moment, that is all that really matters. Feel the spirit that is within your body trying to tell you to calm down, relax and connect to nature: clean and store away human conflict, fear, adversity and unrealistic thoughts of the end of the world.

I feel the spirit say, "Humans may have to face many catastrophes and adversities on Earth, but it is natural. Many of these crises are lessons; however, the world will never come to an end. Do not let this rumor, or so called prediction, influence you. Humans must stop casting their wishes on negative events because thoughts and thought-words have the power to transcend into the air: when energy echoes back, it will transfer into its physical equivalent as each individual wishes. Therefore, humans should always be careful what they wish for... Humans must live in consciousness now, in the timeless present, and clear a state of thoughtlessness and constantly build the relationship from within and choose to live in consciousness now. Observe and monitor every human life, each will improve and change and feel the God-realization and be conscious of His presence and, more importantly, be conscious of each thought cast into the atmosphere with compassion and love. For individuals, as you begin reach out for the spirit now to assist your life and pay deep attention to your inner body and begin to realize your own Inner Source, you return home to the void. Then you know everything in the physical world is only temporary: you resume your infinite identity and surrender to what is. You live in the past, a life situation, and you will live in the future. But, you will not be the same person you were before. You will just continue to evolve and your spirit is ever-lasting and always-developing until it returns home to the Universal Source. On Earth, you are a bridge between the Inner Source, the spiritual realm and God and the world. It is the state of consciousness or enlightenment. Remember life on Earth is a continuum and there will be no end unless God says so: until then, live well and be well and many blessings to EARTH from God."

Chapter Twenty Four
Know yourself

Do we really know ourselves or have we really met the enemy and they are us? Indeed, we are our own enemies, do you know that? Sometimes we love ourselves, but for a while we are not so sure. It is confusing: you thought perhaps you have a spiteful mind. Oh no, you hope not. Relax: it is just your negative emotional thoughts that cause this bewilderment in the mind that affects you so your mood wavers, is indecisive and fluctuates from the time to time and rises and falls, but it is not someone else's problem. This is something you can come to know in yourself. But, you have met the Ego friend that is *you*. The more you make friends with your false self, the more you see that your ways of handling things are so irresponsible and rooted in mistaken thinking in order to make your gloomy self happy to avoid problems and blame somebody else.

You are a little uncertain and puzzled as to who is your real self is and who is your false self. You are a great guy who does a lot of work with the homeless in Seattle, yet you have not been into the homeless area society rejected. Although you work with the homeless, are you willing to go into that area? That is the only way to work with these parts of your real self and override your Ego that is rebuffed. It's all interconnected and interrelated.

A script is written for artists to act and play in the theater, but in reality the script can be fitted into your and everyone's life. The script reflects the reality of our society in real time. We heal ourselves in order to heal others; however, we heal others in order to heal ourselves. When we begin to heal somebody, somehow we end up healing ourselves in consciousness. If we truly want to be there for other people and help them wholeheartedly and without holding back from anybody, it must all be craved from our spiritual heart, then our own self-image of how kind our compassionate and lovely our heart is gets blown away. We are being tested and always pass our requisite level and match in the contest. The more you meet your match, the more you feel excited and want to do more to help others: through the urges of your kind heart, you just cannot deny the truth that is the infinite side of your real self that inspires you to do what you need to do. However, you cannot do it without going out of your comfort zone: you have to go out there to meet everyone and add more ingredients to your dishes of not defying anybody or anything in your heart. You need to explore in reality and go deeper with your true kindness and loveliness because it is the only way you see it all of your real self and know thyself.

Every time you face challenges, it is as though your button gets pushed, showing your false self in the mirror: you see it all and also deny it all. It is as though you were asking the mirror to tell you what you want to hear: whether you have been kind or unkind to others or been selfish. In some way, you can even use your instinct to convey yourself to your limitations, to make you feel you are doing better. What we do not want to hear is any negative comment from the mirror. Nonetheless, there is no point really blaming the mirror for telling the truth or even condemning the mirror for showing your real self.

When we do not want any undesired feedback from others, we do not want to expose the truth, so we cover it up. But, if you try to cover things up that you do not want others to see, you are shocked and offended when it turns out everyone finds out anyway. The point is that you try to protect yourself is strong enough, all-powerful and convincing.

On the other hand, it may not be an appropriate approach to handling things. You must face and accept the consequences and not fall into the blind spot of your own trap and get hurt. As Jesus said, "You need to seek the truth and the truth will set you free." You must turn around and fix the problem taking all the interests in your life and in your immediate environment: that would be your best incentive and stimulus for keeping your heart open, so you can see what happens in the eyes of people, and face them.

There are principal practices you can do to keep your heart open, communicate to others and change yourself for others. You can obtain this through building a relationship with a spiritual mentor, to practice opening your heart and refuge.

First: you must find yourself a spiritual teacher. A sage is someone who inspires you to come out of the closet to walk on your spiritual path. This person speaks to your heart: you want to build a student-teacher relationship with this person. Trust is essential if you want to enter into a serious relationship with a sage; you must determine to stick with him and he will make a commitment stick with you so both of you attach to each other. The responsibility of a spiritual sage is to guide you and point out your mistakes without keeping back anything. Your false self is going to surface, flowing back to the sage. However, you made the commitment so you must stick with the sage till the end. Although, at some point,you want to terminate your commitment, thus far you just want to keep it going. You understand you have entered a student-teacher relationship with the sage and must commit to it. You prefer a teacher who can pin point your mistakes and tell you what he sees in you from the inside out, but not something you want to hear or see. With a sage, you try all the way to improve and condition yourself to make transformational changes. You practice consciousness in the present and learn everything with him. Your training is related to your daily living. Your spiritual teacher will not recognize your existence, but serve as a mirror so you know where you are stuck. The relationship encourages you to awaken. You also learn to be grateful for everything, but not just your spiritual teacher. So, when you get annoyed, you see your spiritual teacher, when your situation is not encouraging, you see your spiritual teacher. When you see your life uplifted, you see your spiritual teacher. You realize that you know what to do and can begin to relate to the pain of all conscious beings. When you feel happy and joyful, you are willing to share with others and develop a sense of understanding and relationships.

Second: practice and tools. You get support when you see clearly what you do rather than run away from it. You have a lot of encouragement from what you learned from the sage and put it into practice to open your heart, further extending your openness to other cognizant beings. You practice breathing joy and are blissful for all. When you feel happy, it occurs to you that you also wish other beings to feel happy.

Third: take refuge. Let's review what you learn from a spiritual teacher to change your personality and enhance your daily activities and transform your conscious present in the now and love for others as much as you love yourself. You learn to let go of everything, without holding onto yourself, and you give it all to others. The second element of practice is to get tools to open your inner consciousness. The third principal is taking refuge. Your shelter is your refuge and food to nourish your body and soul. You learn knowledge and intelligence from your teacher. Your aptitude guides you to explore and question why humans suffer. In other word, we have all the tools that we need to open our hearts, and to work with others in a candid way. We are fortunate enough to have good refuges and never suffer from shortages of anything, as in some other remote parts of the world. We are lucky enough not to have been born in a war zone, with bullets flying around everywhere, all the time, unceasingly. On the contrary, we have a comfortable human life in North America, or in Britain: we grow up with almost everything within our reach and no shortages. Therefore, we should practice sharing with a country in a poor region and send out happiness and joy, showing them that we care about their lives and want them to be happy too. At all time we should show our gratitude for what we have received from the Universal Source and continually practice every moment of our life and feel grateful and appreciative for all the things that happen to us and never cease.

It is time to do things wholeheartedly, without worrying about anything; we should just go for it and do it. You may find it risky or you may feel the need to get out of your comfort zone or even risk your life. You observe your compassionate heart: you are aware you can do it and change yourself for others. So, even risk your own life to save the lives of others. It is painful, but you take breaths in and think of all of the other people who are experiencing pain and send out wishes for all people to have a joyful life.

We cannot really help others if we do things through pride and demand things according to our claims. You must understand that you cannot control what another does, even when they reap negative or positive emotions. Most people know what they are doing with a lucid mind, unless they are unconscious then they do not know how they get what they are receiving. That is the reason why many of them believe they are the victims. They do not know how they invited it all through the thought of their intentions which were out of touch with them. Perhaps they are still trying and are really trying to do better— we must not push it. We must leave them alone so they can have room to breathe and make transformational changes of their own accord and in their time.

If another invites us to help them, we must let go of all of our pride without prejudice or judgment: everything has to go to help them wholeheartedly as we follow our hearts. We do it right, as we walk to walk and talk to talk and do a really good job.

The next thing we should not do is compare ourselves with others. Each individual is unique. The uniqueness of individuals means each has different talents, aptitudes, wisdom and intelligence. When we come to knowledge, language and skill, if we do not know, we do not need to know everything. In fact, it is nothing to be ashamed of when we declare we know nothing, withdraw and humble ourselves. Then, you win the trust and respect of others.

We understand from knowledge and experience that we learn and this is part of us and will be with us for long time, till at death we depart. However, we should not keep it and let it go and not capture or retain any for ourselves, but pass it on to the new generation: so you can relax your mind and it happens by detachment, it happens by inspiration and a yearning to want communicate with yourself and others. Ultimately, we all find our own path. Allowing others to do things of their own accord is to obey the Universal Laws of Allowing. We are creators of our own lives and High Consciousness Infinite Selves. We live independently and digest everything and make an impossible thing becomes possible of our own free will. We master our own domain and all that is powerful.

Chapter Twenty Five
Happiness

What is happiness? How do we activate the power of happiness in our lives? Do you have the picture or image of happiness in your mind?

Happiness needs to be triggered and must be felt through positive emotions, then we know that we are happy. It is different from unhappiness or sadness that can occur at any moment or can be influenced by the external environment that causes the chemical exchange in our brains to affect our mood changes in the mind. All of sudden we feel unsafe, disquieted, distressed, angry, anxiety or pain, grief or upset for no known reason. Then, we know that we are not happy. However, you probably recognize these are negative symptoms or images or ego-dictated goals and desires. Yet, some people transform these poisons and utilize them to train their minds and observe each of the negative poisons in whatever form and transform them into their lessons. They collect these negative ingredients into one basket and take breaths in to activate the compassionate heart to subdue these negative activities and exhale to cancel them in their minds without acting them out.

True happiness is based on your life's purpose, your external and internal conditions must be met through training of the mind and your heart, but, most importantly, it is determined by you.

What is your life's purpose? We come here on a mission to learn lessons and fulfill a purpose on Earth. However, since we are unique, therefore individuals are given talents, aptitudes, intelligence, knowledge and wisdom to work with on their own journey. As soon as you arrive here, you may not remember what you do with your life. But, deep inside, you know what your life's purpose is to guide you through so your purpose can be fulfilled. When you work on your purpose, you feel gratification, you feel joy and bliss expressed from the inside to transcend to the external environment, showing that you are on the right track in helping and serving others. Your happiness can be seen on your face, showing that you are happy. True happiness cannot be faked because you are truly happy. You have found the work you love, you are passionate and keen about it. You are serving your country, your fellow man, helping them to develop and evolve and, with your help, they are happy and have gained success and are making transformational changes in their lives so they reflect the joy and happiness back to you. You are happy for them, more than for your own success and gain.

Achieving the inner-awareness of the conscious moment with the vibration of your Source is the foundation to your happiness in consciousness in the present and a deliberate creation of your own life. Feeling the thought you are having now and the thought that you have with your Inner Source, you are aware of your own emotions. Your deliberately created thoughts cause the balance of the two thoughts in alignment, you experience the balance of energy and you are consciously aligned with your own Inner Self. From the state of balanced energy, you immediately experience clarity, physical well-being, abundance in everything you consider to be good, and consistently experience an excited state of joy. This is the state of who-you-really—are.

When you enter this physical life's body, in reality you did not come with any problems, but with a perfect condition, so you could walk on a life journey here. Your presence is to create a life that suits your purpose here. You may come here with a particular skill or talent to make your life on Earth easier. You know that you can have a variety of life choices to fit into your personal preferences, whether big or small, they will be answered by you and you alone in consciousness in the now. Nobody can answer for you because it is your life and it must be created by you and tailored for you. So it will not be in contrast with the environment for you to consciously experience the continuum of who-you-really-are.

By finding one thing that makes you happy, when you contemplate about it, focus upon it until the Law of Magnetic Energy attracts it to you. The more you think about it, the more positive energy will come forth so it is easier for your desire to be converted into profound reality. So, it is up to you to decide which direction matters to you by consciously and deliberately making the decision of which flow you want to follow.

We can cultivate true happiness through the practice of loving kindness, peacefulness, forgiveness and sharing with others without holding back in consciousness in the Now. When we understand each other's differences, that brings out forgiveness to one another. We all make mistakes: some of our actions make other suffer, but some of others' actions have made us suffer. We want to be forgiving and to start afresh. You crave this message into the air through time—space: reality you say, "I now forgive those who wronged me in the past. I fully comprehend that you were suffering and did not see clearly. I no longer feel anger toward you." You must do it intentionally with love and kindness. Once you send out this message you take breaths in of compassion and send out kindness to that person and relinquish to the conscious present and consider the matter is softened and melted into infinity.

We express our love and care for others by spending time with them. True love needs us to be aware. We have to take time to acknowledge the presence of a person we love, "My love, I know you are there, I love you and am always thinking about you." This cannot be done if you are not really consciously present for the person you truly love. We need to acknowledge the presence of our loved one, we have to practice our true presence in the here and now. When we spend time with the person we love, it is to show full love and genuine generosity. The genuine gift that we can offer to others is our true presence.

We practice peace by touching our body. If you take a moment to touch our eyes deeply, we will feel joy and peace. By touching each part of our body in awareness, we make peace with our body and we can do the same with our emotions. If there are inner conflicts within us, it is important for us to look within to find out our deeper feelings before the problems get worse and affect others around us. Meditation is one of the practical tools we can use to find out the wars inside us. Through awareness, present in the now, we can calm ourselves down and understand the root of the problem and bring stillness back to the conflicting elements inside us. However, if we can find out methods to touch joy, tranquility and happiness that are already within us, we will live healthy and bold lives and possibly be a resource for others.

Sharing is the most joyous and blissful thing that we give to ourselves. We find happiness through sharing our knowledge, wisdoms and services with others. It brings us profound happiness and inner bliss that we could not find anywhere else. We know that others' needs have been met because of our genuine gifts that we offer to them. You are willing to share your wealth with others because you are grateful and gratified by what you have received from the Universe and live a wonderful, blessed life. So, in order to show your gratefulness, you give away your wealth without holding back to yourself because you recognize the Universal Laws of Detachment. This causes energy exchanges in the Universe that allow the life-flowing energy continue to flow infinitely.

Finally, giving wealth, services and knowledge to help others is the real way to achieve happiness and have abundance circle back to us. We should go beyond the inner dialogue by asking this question, "How can I help you instead of wondering what is in it for me?" Any deed and cause of action that we do will transcend into the Universe and return to us to become our own vision. We are like space ships: anything that we carry into the black space of the Universe will reach the Source and the space ship will return to planet Earth transferring everything to become each individual's reality. If we keep our mind's eyes open, we will see through all the illusion of our conditioning so that our path becomes clear and it will be blessed from the depths of our awareness in the now.

Happiness can be attained through intentionally seeking the mindfulness of your Higher Consciousness Self through spiritual practice and discovering your infinity, giving service to humanity, and finding out your unique talents through service to humanity. When you put the above into practice, you can generate unlimited wealth and abundance. You begin to experience miracles occurring in your life, not just occasionally, but frequently. You will know true joy and happiness and the true meaning of success and the true purpose of life.

Ask yourself daily, "How can I serve others to the best of my knowledge?" and "How can I help others?" The answer is you serve your fellow countrymen with love and compassion. When it comes to real happiness, one can slowly eliminate those factors which lead to pain and suffering and endorsing those which lead to happiness. That is the best way to achieve happiness.

In our world, each day many newborns come into this world, the majority of them can stay, but not all: some of them have as their destiny only to live a few days, maybe weeks, then sadly they have to leave due to illness or other misfortunes. Others are destined to push through to the century and experience every taste life has to offer: joy, victory, triumph, failure, sadness, adversity, love, kindness and compassion. Still, life is unexpected until the very end. However, whether we live a week, a month, or live a very long time, a question remains to be answered: what is the purpose of our life? What is the true meaning of our existence? The purpose of our existence is to seek happiness. As soon as we identify the purpose of our life, which is to seek happiness, then it is a positive vision: we must possess and cultivate in our minds steps toward achieving the goal and desire of happiness. We will then know where to search for happiness and obtain the benefits of happiness and offer them to friends and family, but also to the world at large, so that everyone will benefit.

Finally, happiness can also be achieved at every level of our life, even we are facing a midnight crisis or are stuck by catastrophic events, such as serious ill health: all can be modified and adjusted, at least to some degree, so you will see smiles on faces. We can work with our minds to enhance our feelings of moment-to-moment happiness: this is determined by our vista. In fact, our happiness or sadness at any given moment often has little to do with current conditions, but rather it is to do with how we perceive our situation and how gratified we are with what we possess.

Chapter Twenty Six

Manifestation and Re-manifestation:
Faith and God's Healing Power
and Christ's consciousness

Do you believe in reincarnation? It seems that some people in North America and Europe believe in some form of rebirth. For some reason, we believe that there must be an upcoming life so that those who acted improperly in this present life will have to pay for their Karmic debts and misconduct. On the contrary, we may think that this life is too short—we would like to return and try it again. Perhaps, we do not want to die and want to live for eternity. Possibly we like the idea of being able to keep everything such as our aptitudes, our wealth and the good life, just replacing the old with a new body, so that when we do come back than we do not need to redo everything again—we simply carry on. The question is, will we come back? How do we come back and when and from where? Or do we really want to return?

Perhaps we may have lived many lives before we come to this life. Conceivably, if we are a re-manifestation once, we might be a re-manifestation twice or more ("Re-manifestation" means that something already existed in other forms in the Universe, for example flowers per-existed as seeds, soil, sunshine and water: when these conditions are met, they simply re-manifested into whatever form needed to be as flower). When a flower has manifested itself, we consider it as born, but if the conditions of the flower are no longer met, we regard the flower as ceased. In fact, the flower is not really dead, it just transformed into different elements to return to its original place, since its presence is not needed. When we transcend thought of birth, death and re-manifestation, then we know everything is a continuum and there is no beginning and no end. It is as when a tree's leaves are falling during the winter season: when spring approaches, the leaves are re-manifested on tree again. It is a circle of energy exchange which temporarily turns energy into other elements and then, when conditions are sufficient, it is capable of being alive by itself. It simply transforms nothing into nothing then from nothing into something (Birth is from nothing transforming into something and death is from something transforming into becoming nothing. In other words, emptiness is emptiness and emptiness comes from the void.).

We should always dwell in the present moment, in the now, and only the now can bring our mindfulness to the present moment. Everything will happen in the present, but nothing will occur again in the past, so it cannot harm you unless you allow it or nothing will ever happen in the future but through the present.

If we are mindful, then we know that the energy of Christ is manifested within us. In fact, Christ's energy can be obtained through daily practice to strengthen and increase our belief in His presence. We do not need to wait for His second coming as you can feel His presence right now. Each moment is a renewal moment. We change moment to moment but the energy of Christ Jesus in us has never changed. It is always present in consciousness in the Now. You connect with Christ's energy within by feeling and sensing it. If you have sense enough to believe it, you will go forth from the presence of God free in body, mind and spirit—healed from within to the outside. When you are conscious of Christ's presence, you request healing and you command in His name that you will be healed. You repent your lack of forgiveness when you come to God for healing with a regretful repentance and the confession of your blunders. Then, if you believe, you can be healed. God wants you to believe now. Your healing progress will begin and in time you will see your body being healed by the power of God and Christ's healing energy presence.

In fact, Buddha's and Christ's teaching are concerned with peace and happiness. It is about the practice of mindfulness present in the now. It is about the Art of Living and attaining joy in every moment in our lives and being mindful of the environment surrounding you. Love yourself as well as you love your neighbor, conscious of your thoughts and emotions. Listen to and get in touch with nature, observe the trees, hear the birds singing as, through these, we can get in touch with the living Buddha, always available, like the dynamic energy of Christ. Christ is the Light, the Truth and the Way. Buddha is the beam of Light that dwells in everyone's heart. Therefore, when Buddha and Christ are here, no darkness can emerge as they wash out every fear in your mind and they are the Light's presence in our hearts.

We worship and love our God and we know God is love, wisdom, power, and mindfulness. However, we reach our beloved God through Christ. We are aware that Christ's consciousness is present in our hearts. Christ is the bridge by which we reach God. If the Kingdom of God is here in the Now, then the energy of Christ can help us enter the Kingdom of God.

If the Kingdom of God is the seed that we seek, then God is what we sow to attain results. God is present in everyone's heart. God is within our consciousness or Buddha is the seed of mindfulness. So, if we are mindful, then we are inevitably aware that the joy in our heart is the presence of God. When in God's presence, we feel joy, true peace and tranquility within and nothing can be compared to it. Once you have been touched by God, you realize that all the things you considered able to bring you joy and happiness have become meaningless to you. Those things may be your obstacles and you detach from them without holding back or reserve. We were looking for joy and happiness all of the time in the past because we did not know where to seek it, but now it is found. Our joy and happiness is within us and no other place or any material thing can promise us an eternity of joy. In the Kingdom of God and only by being united with God do we find ultimate reality. You are no longer afraid of fear. You are no longer afraid of life and death. You are able to let go of all fear because you have already found the truth and the truth is in your spiritual heart. You and the Source are always united and have never separated, but you have to believe and accept what is and feel from your spiritual heart that God is there now.

God wants you to be healed and He always watches over your shoulders to make sure everything is fine: the moment you believe, you will be healed (Isaiah 53: 1-2 and 5: Who would have believed what we heard? Who swathe Lord's power in this? He grew up like a small plant before the Lord, like a root growing in a dry land. 53:5: But he was wounded for the wrong we did; he was crushed for the evil we did. The punishment, which made us well, was given to him.).

God wants us to have faith in the now. He wants to remove you from the Land of the sick and put you in the Land of the saved. When you are saved, you are saved the moment you believe. With God, all things are possible (Mark 9: 23).

Look for Christ's consciousness. His presence heals your physical body. Focus on Jesus and release your faith. Now place your hand on the part of your body that needs healing and begin to praise God for it (Mark 10:27: Jesus said, "What things sow your desire, when you pray, believe that you shall receive them, and you shall have them." Mark 11:24:…with men it is impossible, but not with God: for with God, all things are possible. Mark 10:27: Jesus healed all who came to Him in Faith). I cast out all doubt and come to him now. I trust His healing power will be released into my life. You must believe in Him and you will be healed, with or without His presence, and He always acts upon His promise. You command in Jesus' name: we have peace upon us and, with His power, we are healed.

Suffix

Pain and suffering are depressing, but these two negative poisons have been embedded in our minds since the beginning of time and, no matter where we are or what we are doing, we are surrounded by pain and suffering. In fact, we are vibrated and surrounded by these half-hearted energies, no matter how hard we try to shield ourselves from them. These two poisonous ingredients are a universal reality and factual. They are not a punishment for your blunders, it is not for that reason that you suffer from bodily pain: it is inescapable. The good news is this all shall pass. Everything has a beginning and an end and nothing in the illusion of the physical material world will be everlasting. When pain ends, you are liberated from the energy that bound parts of your life. The moment when these two poisons are detached from us, automatically we feel at ease and relieved.

Embrace your pain with consciousness; accept everything as it is, without judgment. Take breaths in and breaths out through your nostrils with a relaxed mind and contemplate thoughtlessness. Allow nothing to be in the mind in the moment and do nothing and do not attempt to achieve anything: simply relax and be. Let thoughts come to you naturally without forcing them. Trust that everything is perfectly fine and still. Rest your heart and mind and refill your energy so you are aligned with the Universal Source via your natural breaths in, with compassion and kindness, and send out love, peace and harmony. You do not need to experience anything to achieve something, rather let things fall into place naturally without struggles or a fight. Let it all be and get into harness: the vulnerable mind is now contented and tamed and is set to comply with your commands and fulfill your heart's desire.

By connecting the energy with everything that exists, you are extended to the Universal truth and will gain development and growth and further promote your spiritual end. It allows the flow of life's energy to continue to flow and exchange and give benefits to all.

I believe that sometimes we must learn the hard way that without the pain and the irritation, knowledge of wisdom will not be created and manifested inside us. I believe the wisdom of self-advancing systemic training is real: no pain, no transformative gain. Obstacles, pains and suffering manifest as an aspiration for spiritual enlightenment, which ultimately leads us to our paths of awakening and freedom. Pain and suffering will open new perspectives and the harshness of pain gives birth to a whole new notion and inspiration of being: although it is painful, at the end of the tunnel we will see a silver lining transcend us and that is the most fulfilling and enjoyable thing of all.

We must face and embrace our difficulties and perplexities realistically rather than avoiding them and then abundance can be yours. When pain, suffering and misfortunate occurs, we can meditate on being patient, tolerant, our forgiveness of others, and allowing and genuinely accepting that what is we cannot change: we need to be consciously aware that everything takes time to heal and patience is needed to endure adversity in life so we lucidly guide ourselves to dwell in consciousness in the timeless present and sit down quietly and meditate on the omnipresence of God and pray to God. By practicing gratitude and patience, this will help us to bear pain and sorrow, even though it takes a lot of effort, but at the end we will feel real joy, we will be lightened up with laugher: it is worth being patient for long-term success and abundance so we eliminate pain and live life painlessly without regret.

May all who are sick and ill
Quickly be freed from their illness
And may every disease in the world
Never occur again
As long as space endures
As long as there are beings to be found
May I continue likewise to remain
To soothe the sufferings of all living beings
—Dalai Lama

Prayer, chanting mantra and visualizations help us heal. It heals the imbalance of our energy both internal and external blend to restore the natural state of Infinite and finite being through spiritual-realization, mindfulness, awaken and life enlightened to consciousness in the here and now.

The healing manta of the Medicine Buddha is:

TA—YA—TA OM BEKANZE BEKANZE MAHABEKANZE KADZA SUMUD—GATE SOHA

Awakening to the Power of God
Trigger the Power from within
Relinquish to the person you were
Free and purify your breathe in and breathe out through
your nostrils
Let the Swan help your spirit to transcend to the outer
limits
—HW

~The End~